## Table of Contents

A Symphony of Sorrow and Spectacle.........6
The Cyclical Tragedy of the Smith Family 12
...................................................................27
The Genesis of DJ Shadowblade.................27
Cyrax's Musical Misadventures..................33
   Cyrax's Descent into Digital Infamy......39
...................................................................43
The Quiet Years..........................................44
The Descent into Digital Delusions............49
Chuck Steagle Saga....................................58
The Darkening Spiral..................................67
The Living Room Saga................................73
Cyrax's Late 2017 Spiral.............................82
The Delusions Deepen: Cyrax's Descent into Fantasy.................................................86
The D pics – The Road to Lolcow...............91
Delusions of Grandeur: Cyrax's Summer of Discontent...................................................96
Wrapping up 2018....................................109
...................................................................112
The Candle Inferno...................................113
The Reborn Records Reckoning: Cyrax's Collision with Reality.................................119
Shadows of the Past: Cyrax's Carceral Confession................................................124

Cyrax's February Fury..................................133
Fred and The Tree Incident........................137
The Ascent to Infamy: Cyrax's Troll Infestation................................................142
The Great Label Trolling Saga....................146
The Descent into Chaos.............................152
A New Year of Digital Debauchery............156
Cyrax's Return and Relationship Implosion
........................................................................164
........................................................................168
Cyrax's Violent Tendencies Exposed.........169
The Summer of Delusion............................173
A Demonic Ending to 2020........................177
A New Year Of Spiraling..............................184
March Madness............................................188
........................................................................191
The Great Stylus Incident...........................192
Cyrax's Darkest Hour..................................196
Redemption and Relapse...........................201
........................................................................205
Cyrax's Edless Spiral....................................206
The LolcowLive Spectacle..........................216
The Final Confrontation: Cyrax's Last Stand................................................................233
........................................................................237
Cyrax's Legacy and the Digital Age..........238

2

This is a work of fiction. Names, characters, places and incidents either are products of the author's imagination or are used fictitiously.

## A Symphony of Sorrow and Spectacle

In the annals of internet infamy, few figures have struck such a discordant chord as Patrick Smith, better known by his online moniker "Cyrax." Born on September 20, 1990, in the heartland of Ohio, Cyrax's life began as a fragile whisper, barely audible against the cacophony of a world that seemed determined to drown him out from the very start.

Picture, if you will, a newborn so delicate that he could have been cradled in the palm of your hand. Weighing a mere 1 pound and 12 ounces, Patrick entered this world at just 26 weeks gestation, his tiny form a testament to the precarious nature of his existence. With only one fully functioning kidney, a lung and a half, and a single eye that refused to focus properly, it was as if fate itself had conspired to stack the deck against him.

But the true architect of Patrick's challenging beginnings was not some cosmic dealer, but rather the very woman who brought him into this world. Connie Lobdell, Cyrax's mother, was herself a soul adrift in a sea of cognitive challenges. While the full extent of her disabilities remains shrouded in mystery, the whispers of family members paint a picture of a woman ill-equipped for the monumental task of motherhood.

Sally, Patrick's grandmother, would later claim that Connie was "fully disabled," a vague descriptor that raises more questions than it answers. What demons lurked in the shadows of Connie's mind? What invisible barriers separated her from the neurotypical world around her? These are questions that may never find satisfactory answers, lost to the mists of time and the fog of family secrets.

Patrick's father, a man whose name has been carefully excised from the public record, offered a slightly more illuminating glimpse into Connie's condition. He spoke of ADHD, that modern-day catch-all for minds that refuse to march to society's drumbeat. But there was something more, an unnamed specter that haunted Connie's cognitive landscape. Whatever this mysterious affliction may have been, its effects were profound. The father recounted, with a mixture of patience and exasperation, how it took him three long years to teach Connie the seemingly simple task of operating a motor vehicle.

As the details of Patrick's origins came to light, whispers began to circulate through the darkest corners of the internet. Could Cyrax be yet another victim of that insidious saboteur of fetal development, alcohol? The specter of Fetal Alcohol Syndrome loomed large in these discussions, a tantalizing explanation for the constellation of physical and cognitive challenges that would come to define Patrick's life.

Yet, even as these rumors swirled, a sobering reality emerged. If Connie had indeed imbibed during her pregnancy, how could one truly hold her accountable? The very cognitive limitations that may have led her to make such a devastating choice also render her, in the eyes of many, incapable of fully comprehending the consequences of her actions. It's a moral quandary that would make even the most steadfast ethicist pause, a Gordian knot of culpability and compassion.

But what of Patrick's father, that enigmatic figure lurking in the background of this tragic tableau? Unlike Connie, he appears to have been of sound mind, a neurotypical navigator in the stormy seas of Patrick's early life. Yet, as we shall see, his role in this unfolding drama is far from straightforward, a complex interplay of responsibility and abdication that would shape the course of Patrick's life in ways both subtle and profound.

As we delve deeper into the twisted tale of Cyrax, we must ask ourselves: at what point does nature give way to nurture? When do the cards we're dealt at birth become less important than how we choose to play them? These are questions that will haunt us as we explore the life and times of Patrick "Cyrax" Smith, a man whose journey from fragile infant to internet pariah serves as a stark reminder of the thin line between victim and villain in our increasingly interconnected world.

In the chapters to come, we will peel back the layers of Cyrax's life, examining the pivotal moments and fateful decisions that transformed a struggling young man into a figure of both pity and revulsion. We'll explore his ill-fated forays into the world of music, his tumultuous relationships with family and strangers alike, and the series of increasingly disturbing incidents that have led him to the brink of legal ruin.

# The Cyclical Tragedy of the Smith Family

In the annals of human depravity, few stories are as harrowing as that of the Smith family. Their tale is a generational saga of abuse, misfortune, and the perpetuation of trauma that reads like a Faulknerian nightmare set against the backdrop of modern America. At the center of this maelstrom stands Patrick "Cyrax" Smith, a man whose life was shaped by forces beyond his control long before he drew his first breath.

The year was 1994, and the quiet streets of Alaska were about to be rocked by a crime that would cast a long shadow over the Smith family for decades to come. Ruple Mark Smith, the man who would later be known as Cyrax Senior, found himself in the crosshairs of the law. While accounts of the exact timing vary – Cyrax himself claims his father was incarcerated on the very day of his birth – official records suggest that the arrest occurred when young Patrick was a mere toddler, somewhere between three and four years old.

On that fateful day of July 26th, a 14-year-old girl's life was irreparably altered. She was violently wrenched from her bicycle and dragged into the depths of a nightmare that would haunt her for years to come. The assailant, a predator who had been stalking his prey with the patience of a jungle cat, chased her for a terrifying 50 feet before committing his heinous act. This wasn't a crime of opportunity or passion; it was a meticulously planned attack that hinted at a darker history of similar transgressions.

The young victim, whose name has been mercifully withheld from the public eye, provided a detailed description of her attacker to the authorities. She spoke of his appearance, his mannerisms, and most crucially, his distinctive blue 10-speed bicycle. Armed with this information, law enforcement crafted a composite sketch that would prove to be the key to unlocking this grim mystery.

In a twist of fate that would be almost comical if it weren't so tragic, the composite sketch found its way into the local newspaper. And who should happen upon this illustrated likeness of evil but Ruple Smith himself, a mere 48 hours after the attack. It was at this moment that the infamous Smith family intellect – or lack thereof – made its grand debut on the stage of criminal justice.

In a move that can only be described as breathtakingly foolish, Ruple decided to contact the police of his own volition. His ill-conceived plan? To point out the uncanny resemblance between himself and the sketch, all while vehemently denying any involvement in the crime. It was as if he believed that by acknowledging the similarity, he could somehow inoculate himself against suspicion.

Needless to say, this strategy backfired spectacularly. The officer who took Ruple's call was immediately struck by the oddity of the situation and promptly reported it to their superior. Before long, a squad car was dispatched to Ruple's residence, setting in motion a chain of events that would alter the course of the Smith family forever.

As the responding officer pulled up to Ruple's home, their eyes were immediately drawn to a sight that sent a chill down their spine: there, in plain view, stood a blue 10-speed bicycle – an exact match for the one described by the victim. It was as if Ruple had gift-wrapped the evidence and left it on his front lawn for all to see.

Under the weight of mounting evidence and increasingly pointed questions, Ruple's facade began to crumble. While he stopped short of an outright confession to the sexual assault, he made statements that amounted to an admission of kidnapping. He spoke of dragging the victim across the road against her will, each word another nail in the coffin of his freedom.

It was at this point that Ruple, perhaps finally realizing the gravity of his situation, requested legal counsel. But the damage had been done. His ill-advised statements, coupled with the damning physical evidence, were more than enough to justify an arrest and subsequent trial.

In the courtroom, Ruple's fate was sealed. A jury, presented with the overwhelming evidence of his guilt, found him guilty on all counts: kidnapping, sexual assault, and the sexual abuse of a minor. In a last-ditch effort to evade justice, Ruple attempted to appeal his convictions. But the wheels of justice, once set in motion, proved unstoppable. His appeals were denied, and Ruple Mark Smith was sentenced to serve two decades behind bars.

The repercussions of Ruple's actions extended far beyond his own life. With Cyrax Senior locked away and Connie Lobdell deemed unfit to care for a child due to her cognitive limitations, young Patrick found himself adrift in a sea of uncertainty. It was in this moment of crisis that Sally, Patrick's grandmother, stepped forward to assume the mantle of caregiver.

Sally made the decision to uproot Patrick from the cold expanse of Alaska, transplanting him to the more temperate climes of Akron, Ohio. It was a move born of necessity, but one that would shape the course of Patrick's life in ways that no one could have predicted.

But as we delve deeper into the Smith family history, we uncover a pattern of abuse and exploitation that spans generations. Sally, it turns out, was no stranger to the kind of trauma that had befallen her grandson's victim. In a cruel twist of fate, she had found herself in a strikingly similar situation, albeit on the receiving end of such abuse.

Public records and local newspaper articles paint a disturbing picture of Sally's early life. Born in 1952, she was a mere child of 14 when she was wed to William "Bill" Smith, a man 11 years her senior. By the time she gave birth to Ruple in 1969, Sally was still only 17 – a child herself, thrust into the role of mother by a man old enough to know better.

The parallels between Sally's experience and the crime committed by her son Ruple are chilling. Both involved 14-year-old girls and men in their mid-twenties. It's a pattern of abuse that seems to echo through the Smith family line, a generational curse that Patrick "Cyrax" Smith would inherit through no fault of his own.

As if this family saga wasn't tragic enough, we learn of yet another character in this grim play: another Bill Smith, Ruple's older brother. His story, while less sensational than that of his brother, is no less heartbreaking. Stricken with both AIDS and cancer, Bill fought a losing battle against his failing body until he finally succumbed to his illnesses in 2015.

This is how we get to Chance James Finley Wilkins, better known to the digital world as Cyrax. His story is a tapestry woven from threads of tragedy, transformation, and alleged transgression, set against the backdrop of turn-of-the-millennium America. To truly understand the man who would become Cyrax, we must first delve into the crucible of his youth, where the forces that would shape his destiny first began to coalesce.

The tale begins with a name change, a seemingly innocuous act that would come to symbolize the constant flux of Cyrax's identity. Born Patrick Smith, the young boy found himself rechristened as Chance Wilkins when his grandmother, Sally, assumed guardianship. Sally, having married Gordon Wilkins, bestowed upon her ward not just a new name, but a new identity – one that would follow him throughout his tumultuous life.

This transformation was more than nominal; it was geographical as well. Uprooted from the frigid expanses of Alaska, Chance found himself transplanted to the more temperate climes of Akron, Ohio. It was a journey that mirrored the internal upheaval of a child barely five years old, already navigating a world that seemed determined to reshape him at every turn.

In Cyrax's own recollection, his school years were a gauntlet of torment and isolation. He paints a vivid picture of a child mercilessly bullied, subjected to the cruel rituals of adolescent hierarchies. "I was supposed to die the day that I was born," Cyrax would later recount, his voice tinged with a mixture of defiance and resignation. "I was born with one kidney and one and a half lungs. Growing up through school, I got picked on, bullied way more than most. I got judged, beat up every day. I was that kid that was an outcast in high school."

Yet, as with many aspects of Cyrax's narrative, the truth proves to be a more complex tapestry than his recollections would suggest. Enter El Beth, a high school acquaintance whose account paints a markedly different picture of Chance's adolescent years. "We met quite literally in high school," El Beth recalls. "We had a mutual friend in common, and that's how we met."

Far from the isolated pariah Cyrax describes, El Beth's recollections suggest a young man with a circle of friends, united by a shared passion for dance. She speaks of performances at school talent shows, of a piece called "The Dueling Dancers" in which she and Chance took center stage.

While no footage of these performances survives, they stand as testament to a side of Cyrax's youth that he seems reluctant to acknowledge – one of friendship, creativity, and belonging.

At the center of this social circle stood Billy Syler, a figure who would loom large in the Cyrax mythology. Described by Chance as "a closer friend than the rest of the group," Billy was a short, legally blind African-American student who introduced Cyrax to Linkin Park, a band that would become a cornerstone of his musical tastes. The bonds forged in those high school years seemed, on the surface, to be the stuff of typical teenage friendship – shared interests, inside jokes, and the camaraderie of outsiders finding their place in the world.

But as with so many aspects of the Cyrax saga, this seemingly innocuous friendship would later become the subject of intense scrutiny and controversy. Years after his high school days, Cyrax would make a startling claim about his relationship with Billy – an allegation that would send shockwaves through his online following and raise serious questions about the nature of truth in Cyrax's narrative.

"Unfortunately, when I was 16 to 17 years old, around that time period, I was actually [assaulted] by one of my best friends from high school," Cyrax would later state, his tone disturbingly matter-of-fact for such a weighty accusation. "At the time, I didn't know that he was gay. I had actually met this kid, his name was Billy Syler. We had gone to the same high school together, and me and him grew really, really close. We were super cool with each other."

This bombshell allegation, casually dropped into conversation, set off a firestorm of speculation and investigation among Cyrax's followers. The story seemed to shift with each retelling – in one version, Cyrax claimed his family had spoken to the school about the alleged incident, resulting in his own expulsion "so it wouldn't happen again." The timeline, too, proved frustratingly elastic, with Cyrax initially claiming to have been 16 or 17 at the time, only to later adjust his age upward when it was pointed out that he hadn't changed high schools until 2009, when he would have been 19.

The inconsistencies in Cyrax's account, coupled with the serious nature of his allegations, spurred his online followers to action. Armed with the name Billy Syler – a detail Cyrax had freely provided – they set out to uncover the truth. What they found would turn the narrative on its head and cast a long shadow over Cyrax's credibility.

Through social media, Cyrax's followers made contact with Billy Syler himself. What emerged from this communication was a story that stood in stark contrast to Cyrax's claims – a story that, if true, painted Cyrax not as a victim, but as a perpetrator.

According to Billy's account, it was Cyrax who had initiated an unwanted sexual encounter. "We were up in my room, you know, it was late at night, probably 12, 1:00 on a weekday," Billy recounted. "When it gets hot, you know, guys tend to take off their shirts and everything. I was either on my belly on the floor, or I think I was searching for something, and the next thing I know... at this point, I had never given any type of consent whatsoever."

The implications of this revelation were staggering. If Billy's account was to be believed, it suggested that Cyrax, at the age of 18 or 19, had sexually assaulted a disabled minor – a crime of profound severity that stood in direct opposition to the narrative Cyrax had been spinning.

As the 2000s drew to a close, the stage was set for Cyrax's emergence as a figure of internet notoriety. But even as his online presence began to take shape, tragedy continued to dog his personal life. In 2007, on Cyrax's 17th birthday, his mother Connie – who had remarried in 2002 – met a tragic end in a house fire caused by an improperly installed wood stove.

This loss, coming at such a pivotal moment in Cyrax's life, would undoubtedly leave its mark on the man he was becoming

# The Genesis of DJ Shadowblade

The turn of the decade brought little respite for Chance Wilkins, the young man who would soon become known to the internet as Cyrax. In late 2008, barely a year after the tragic loss of his mother, the Wilkins household faced yet another ordeal. Their home, a sanctuary for Chance and his grandmother Sally, was violated by an unknown intruder. The details of this break-in remain shrouded in mystery, with no information available on whether the perpetrator was ever brought to justice.

As the calendar flipped to 2009, Chance took his first tentative steps into the digital realm. With the creation of his inaugural YouTube channel, he began to carve out a space for himself in the vast landscape of the internet. However, these early forays into content creation were hardly groundbreaking. The channel primarily showcased amateur music videos (AMVs) cobbled together using freeware, with a liberal helping of content appropriated from other creators. It was an inauspicious beginning, but one that would set the stage for Cyrax's later, more notorious online presence.

The years 2010 and 2011 passed with relative quietude, at least in terms of public drama. Chance's Facebook posts from this period paint a picture at odds with his later claims of relentless bullying and social isolation. These posts reveal a young man navigating the typical terrain of adolescent romance, boasting of multiple girlfriends and sharing the kind of crude humor that often characterizes teenage social media use. One particularly memorable post read: "Santa ho ho ho me damn Santa has three hoes what a man wh one at a time and they better get paid extra you so fat and old nasty."

However, the relative calm of these years would prove to be the lull before a storm of controversy and legal troubles. In 2012, the tension that had been building in the Wilkins household finally boiled over into violence. On Valentine's Day, a day typically associated with love and affection, the police were called to respond to a domestic disturbance at the Wilkins residence.

The details of this incident, obtained through a Freedom of Information Act request by Cyrax's dedicated followers, paint a disturbing picture. The report, filed by Sally's brother William Arson, describes Chance as "out of control and fighting with his mom." The situation escalated to the point where Chance allegedly attempted to choke or strangle his grandmother before fleeing the house on foot, heading towards the freeway.

While the police report mercifully cites no injuries and no weapons used, the incident marked a dark turning point in Chance's life. The mug shot taken following this altercation serves as a stark visual reminder of this tumultuous period.

It was around this time that Chance began to craft the online persona that would eventually evolve into Cyrax. Under the moniker "DJ Shadowblade" (often misspelled in various creative ways), he started to establish a more significant online presence. One of his early viral attempts was a video purporting to showcase him breaking Chester Bennington's record for the longest scream. In reality, the audio was less a scream and more an elongated groan, prompting one viewer to quip, "Sounds like me when the drive-thru takes longer than 3 minutes."

The following year, despite being 23 years old and still in high school, Chance began posting videos of himself performing basic parkour moves such as handstands and wall jumps. These videos, while unremarkable in terms of skill or execution, hinted at Chance's desire for attention and validation from an online audience.

Chance's academic claims during this period were as grandiose as they were implausible. He asserted that he had maintained a GPA just shy of 4.0 and was at the top of his class, but was denied graduation because he fell short of a perfect GPA and was "too ugly to graduate." He further claimed that this injustice led to his expulsion from the school.

Perhaps the most outlandish of Chance's claims from this period involved an alleged incident of severe bullying. According to his account, a group of students had pushed him from a balcony at school. However, this narrative was swiftly debunked by his aunt in a later interview. She revealed the truth: during lunchtime, Chance had accepted a dare to perform a backflip from the second-floor balcony. The stunt ended predictably poorly, with Chance landing on his side and breaking his arm.

Rather than admit to this act of reckless bravado, Chance concocted a story of victimization. He went so far as to file a false police report, accusing other students of pushing him. When the truth came to light, the consequences were swift and severe. Chance was expelled from the school, his fabricated tale of bullying unraveling in the face of evidence. His actual academic performance, with a GPA reportedly below 1.0, likely contributed to the school's decision.

## Cyrax's Musical Misadventures

As Chance Wilkins entered his early twenties, his online persona began to take shape, marked by a series of exaggerations, fabrications, and ill-fated attempts to break into the music industry. One of the most persistent myths in Cyrax's personal lore was the tale of his "inexplicable talent" – a gift he claimed to have acquired after a supposed head injury from his infamous balcony incident. However, this narrative quickly unravels when faced with the evidence of his early uploads, which clearly show his musical aspirations predating any alleged cranial trauma.

As early as 2012, Chance had already immersed himself in the Juggalo subculture, a community centered around fans of the hip-hop duo Insane Clown Posse (ICP). One of his earliest surviving uploads features a lengthy complaint about the strict rules and expectations within the Juggalo community. This grievance likely stemmed from Chance's superficial engagement with Juggalo culture; he seemed more interested in finding a sense of belonging than genuinely embracing the music and ethos of ICP and their associated acts.

This disconnect became glaringly apparent when a fellow Juggalo decided to test Chance's knowledge of ICP. When asked about his first ICP album, Chance fumbled, vaguely suggesting it might have been either "Jle brothers" or "Riddle Box." When pressed further about the album cover, he deflected, claiming he couldn't remember due to the passage of time. This exchange laid bare the hollowness of Chance's Juggalo identity, revealing him as an imposter within a community known for its inclusive nature.

Despite his tenuous connection to Juggalo culture, Chance continued to claim affiliation with the "family" throughout the following decade. This persistence in the face of obvious incompatibility led one observer to quip, "How dysfunctional do you have to be in order to struggle to meet the criteria for a Juggalo? The only community with lower standards than theirs is probably furries. No offense, just saying."

Chance's online presence during this period was characterized by frequent deletions and new account creations, making it challenging to piece together a comprehensive timeline. However, his LinkedIn page offers some insights, claiming he had been part of a Juggalo record label called "Killer Clown Sounds" since May 2009. His Facebook posts reveal previous occupations as an "abstract artist and painter" at "C Wilkins Art" and, curiously, as a "soldier's son" – likely a reference to his relationship with Gordon

Wilkins, Sally's husband at the time and the source of Chance's new surname.

In 2010, Chance claimed to have released his first album, "Blood on My Hands," under the moniker "Kid Darkness." This musical venture was apparently facilitated by his sister, who connected him with Eric Scrub, the owner of a small label. Scrub, it seems, signed Chance out of pity rather than any discernible talent.

Chance's musical journey took an unexpected turn when he briefly reinvented himself as a Christian rock artist. While concrete evidence of his performances in this genre is scarce, we do have a poster suggesting he played at least one gig. In lieu of actual footage, we're left with Chance's unique expressions of religious fervor, such as this Facebook post: "I swear man I wish I could give that no-good Satan and his demons a piece of my fist and foot in their mouths and shut them up for good." In a comment on the same post, he bizarrely claimed that God had killed the devil at some point – a theological assertion not found in any mainstream Christian doctrine.

As Chance struggled to gain traction in the music industry, his frustration became evident in his social media posts. In one particularly revealing message, he wrote: "My name is Chance Wilkins. I'm 21 years old with my mom working 2 days a week waiting tables in a little restaurant and it's still not being enough to fully get by on bills. And me going through many hardships in life, I decided to do something to help all that so I decided to get into music. And many people have judged me because I autotune my real voice to make it sound better but I don't care I still keep going and I always will. I don't ask for much I just ask for my dream to come true so I can help my family."

This message, while touching in its vulnerability, also hinted at the mounting pressure Chance felt to support his family. It was during this stressful period that he began developing his infamous "skullet" hairstyle – a distinctive look that would become one of his identifying features in the years to come.

Despite the lack of any tangible success, Chance remained convinced that fame and fortune were just around the corner. He believed he was on the verge of earning up to $5,000 and gracing the covers of every music magazine. These delusions of grandeur were entirely self-generated; even before internet trolls began feeding his fantasies with false promises, Chance proved adept at convincing himself of his imminent stardom.

## Cyrax's Descent into Digital Infamy

In 2012, Chance Wilkins, now fully embracing his online persona of Cyrax, continued to document his life through a series of increasingly bizarre and poorly conceived uploads. One such video, aptly titled "Inside the Shadows," offered an unsolicited tour of his living space to a non-existent audience. The video's title proved eerily appropriate, as the abysmal lighting rendered most of the content nearly indiscernible.

While much of Cyrax's early content has been lost to time, likely languishing on the cursed confines of his hard drive, we do have access to one archived song from this period. The track, characterized by the absence of Cyrax's typical slurring drawl and featuring a beat that one critic described as "sounding like a brain hemorrhage converted to MP3," suggests that Cyrax may have been attempting to position himself as a producer rather than a vocalist.

August 2012 saw Cyrax claiming collaboration with a fellow Juggalo rapper named Spitfire the Twisted Killer. However, extensive research has failed to uncover any evidence of this artist's existence, casting doubt on the veracity of Cyrax's claims.

Cyrax's personal life during this period was equally tumultuous. Early 2012 found him apparently involved with a girl named Hannah, to whom he issued a public apology for unspecified transgressions. In a display of performative emotion, he credited Hannah with preventing him from doing "something drastic" the night before. However, this relationship seemed short-lived, as Cyrax soon announced not only a new girlfriend but an engagement to a woman named Heather. She, too, appeared to be deeply entrenched in Juggalo culture, collaborating musically with Cyrax under the moniker Shadow Cat Haslet.

Cyrax's attempts at artistic expression extended beyond music. In late 2012, he announced plans for a manga series titled "Spec Orbs," slated for release in early to mid-2013. Unsurprisingly, this project never materialized.

As time progressed, Chance's behavior became increasingly erratic. Having mastered the absolute basics of music production, he seemed to experience an unwarranted ego boost that he struggled to manage. Early signs of the confrontational behavior that would later define his online presence began to emerge. A clip from early 2013 shows Cyrax addressing someone who allegedly insulted one of his friends, adopting a belligerent tone reminiscent of a WWE wrestler whose gimmick involves speaking as if he'd just emerged from a sludge puddle in a trailer park.

Despite his increasingly unlikable online persona, Cyrax continued to find romantic partners. By 2013, we finally got a glimpse of Heather in a video published on New Year's Day. In this video, Cyrax announced his departure from the Juggalo lifestyle while emphasizing that he still considered himself part of the "family."

Cyrax's attempts to cultivate an air of sophistication were painfully evident in his mimicry of celebrity interview styles. His behavior resembled a sort of real-time cargo cult, imitating the trappings of fame without understanding its substance.

A subsequent video featured Cyrax apologizing for throwing away dog tags from his record label, Killer Clown Sounds. The video's production values were questionable at best, with the sad theme from early Naruto episodes playing in the background and Heather hovering ominously behind Cyrax. In a characteristic move, he subtly shifted blame for the incident onto his grandmother, Sally.

Cyrax's musical endeavors continued to be a source of controversy. Years later, investigations into his departure from Scrub's label revealed a pattern of theft and deception. Eric Scrub, the label owner, stated in an interview: "I've known him for close to maybe 10 years, and to be honest with you, in the beginning, I felt bad for the guy... He used to go by Virus, which was also stolen from me. I don't know, man, he stole like 10 of my songs."

## The Quiet Years

The year 2013 marked a period of relative quiet for Cyrax, particularly in terms of his social media presence. His once-bustling Facebook page dwindled to a handful of posts, suggesting a retreat from the digital limelight or perhaps a shift in his online strategy. Following his departure from Killer Clown Sounds, Cyrax aligned himself with a new musical collective called Redcon 1, though details of this association remain scarce.

The year closed with another police report documenting a domestic disturbance, called in by Sally. The specifics of this incident, like so many in Cyrax's life, remain shrouded in mystery.

As 2014 dawned, Cyrax's online activity took on a more visual nature. While his textual posts remained infrequent, he frequently updated his profile and background pictures with eclectic choices. One such image featured a Second Life character juxtaposed with song lyrics, while another showcased "Red Phoenix," an apparent superhero of Cyrax's own creation. His penchant for the fantastical extended to creating Yu-Gi-Oh style cards for various new metal and emo bands, a curious blend of his musical and gaming interests.

Cyrax's self-proclaimed titles during this period grew increasingly grandiose and disconnected from reality. He styled himself as an "anime illustrator and author" for a non-existent series called "Ren Maru High Clander." More bizarrely, he began referring to himself as an "American Soldier," a claim seemingly rooted in his adoptive father Gordon's military background rather than any actual service of his own.

May 2014 saw the birth of "Gamer Madness Monthly," a video series that, true to Cyrax's form, never progressed beyond its inaugural episode. In this solitary installment, he announced plans for a horror game called "Possessions," which he ambitiously claimed would combine elements of Resident Evil, Call of Duty, and Halo – a feat of game design that exists only in Cyrax's imagination.

Cyrax's attempt to engage with political discourse resulted in a misguided video addressing "Zero Tolerance laws on fighting." His appeal to then-President Barack Obama to change these laws so "people can defend themselves" demonstrated a fundamental misunderstanding of the topic at hand. The irony of his stance was not lost on observers, given that, were it not for his visible challenges, he could have faced assault charges for his earlier altercation with Sally.

After months of silence, Cyrax resurfaced with a new rap track. The cover art indicated a collaboration with an unnamed third party under the group name "Underground Assassins." The track featured a curious mix of styles, including brief segments of nu-metal screaming, likely contributed by Cyrax's mysterious collaborator. Notably, Cyrax's lyrics were peppered liberally with racial slurs, a choice he seemingly justified by claiming to be "from the hood." His vocals appeared to be artificially sped up, yet still managed to be wildly off-beat, all set over a pilfered Linkin Park instrumental.

Concurrent with this musical release, Cyrax launched "Underground Show," yet another video series that, like its predecessors, failed to progress beyond its first episode. The show's premise involved Cyrax reviewing pop culture artifacts from the 1990s and earlier, though it primarily served as a platform for him to showcase his plastic bead art creations.

In a final burst of creative output for the year, Cyrax released a cover of Linkin Park's "Burn It Down," replacing the original vocals with his attempt at grindcore-style screaming. He also uploaded a Juggalo-themed track, though the polished production and pitched-up vocals cast doubt on the extent of Cyrax's involvement in its creation.

As 2014 drew to a close, Cyrax's online presence remained a jumbled mosaic of half-realized projects, misappropriated identities, and musical endeavors of dubious quality. His digital footprint, while less active than in previous years, continued to paint a picture of a man desperately seeking validation and recognition in a world that seemed increasingly disinterested in what he had to offer.

# The Descent into Digital Delusions

As we delve into the labyrinthine twists of Cyrax's digital footprint during the years 2015 and 2016, we find ourselves navigating a landscape fraught with grandiose ambitions, fleeting obsessions, and an ever-present undercurrent of desperation for validation and connection.

The year 2015 dawned with an eerie silence from Cyrax's usual online haunts. This uncharacteristic quiescence, however, was not born of introspection or personal growth, but rather the aftermath of a violent altercation that would cast a long shadow over the months to come. In April, Cyrax found himself embroiled in a physical confrontation that culminated in a brutal collision with a stop sign, allegedly resulting in severe back trauma that necessitated emergency medical intervention.

The incident left more than just physical scars. Cyrax's ego, once inflated by bravado and threats of violence, lay deflated in the wake of this very real encounter with aggression. His online persona, typically marked by bombastic claims of physical prowess, fell silent on the subject of altercations. Instead, a newfound resentment towards law enforcement bubbled to the surface, manifesting in a Facebook post that bemoaned the arrest of his assailant and claimed ongoing spinal misalignment despite medical professionals finding no evidence of lasting injury.

As autumn leaves began to fall, Cyrax attempted to resurrect his musical aspirations. October saw him don the mantle of "professional music producer," offering beats for sale at the bargain-basement price of one dollar each. This venture into the world of commerce proved as ill-fated as his previous artistic endeavors, with a deafening silence from potential buyers serving as a harsh critique of his musical offerings.

The lack of interest in his compositions struck a devastating blow to Cyrax's fragile self-image. In a moment of raw vulnerability, he took to social media to declare his retirement from the music world:

"I hate to say this, but my work as a music artist is done. I know I'm going to upset and piss a lot of you off, but the music world is not where I belong anymore. I don't have the talent I used to have, and I'm sorry for those of you who I'm going to upset with this post, but my future lies in doing my artwork. As of this moment, I am done with music for good. Again, I'm truly sorry for those of you I'm going to make mad and upset, but please try to understand my point."

This dramatic pronouncement, dripping with self-pity and a thinly veiled plea for reassurance, exemplified Cyrax's penchant for emotional extremes. His grandmother, ever the voice of reason in the tempest of his online presence, attempted to contextualize his outburst as a reaction to perceived judgment of his music. However, a more nuanced analysis suggests that Cyrax's fickleness stemmed from a profound inability to sustain focus or commitment, a trait that would manifest repeatedly in his digital exploits.

True to form, Cyrax's "retirement" from music proved as ephemeral as morning dew. Within mere months, he was publicly contemplating the remake of a previous album—an album whose original existence remained shrouded in mystery, much like many of Cyrax's claimed accomplishments.

November brought with it new fixations and frustrations. Cyrax's foray into the world of competitive online gaming via League of Legends ended in ignominy, as he discovered that abandoning matches mid-game resulted in punitive measures.

This digital setback, however, paled in comparison to the baffling development in his personal life: the acquisition of yet another romantic partner.

The internet collective watched in bewildered awe as Cyrax announced his relationship with a woman known only as May—a moniker that may well have been as illusory as many of his other claims. The persistent ability of Cyrax to attract romantic interests, despite his myriad shortcomings and erratic behavior, became a subject of intense speculation among online observers. Some chalked it up to an inexplicable charisma, while others posited more cynical explanations rooted in the peculiarities of his home state's social dynamics.

As the year drew to a close, Cyrax's penchant for inserting himself into unrelated events reached new heights. The tragic shooting of Zach Hussein in a local pizza parlor became fodder for Cyrax's attention-seeking behavior. Despite no discernible connection to the victim, Cyrax inundated social media with posts declaring Hussein his "brother" and "good friend." This macabre spectacle culminated in the creation of custom car designs featuring Hussein's likeness and name, showcased on a hastily constructed Facebook page dubbed "ZNC Customs"—an enterprise undertaken without any apparent consent from Hussein's grieving family.

As 2016 dawned, Cyrax's digital presence evolved into a fever dream of half-baked projects and abandoned ambitions. January alone saw the announcement and swift retraction of plans for an anime-style punk metal band and a mobile video game development venture. These grandiose schemes dissolved into vague promises of manga adaptations, which, like so many of Cyrax's creative endeavors, never materialized.

In a desperate bid for income, Cyrax attempted to monetize his digital detritus, offering a thumb drive laden with purportedly original artwork and unreleased musical compositions for the princely sum of fifty dollars. The artwork, when not outright plagiarized, consisted of rudimentary designs created through automated software, while the musical offerings were little more than the output of beat-generating programs.

February brought with it a return to Cyrax's perennial lament: his lack of a satisfying romantic relationship. In a post dripping with self-pity and specific criteria reminiscent of infamous internet personality Chris Chan, Cyrax bemoaned:

"Why can't I be happy with a wonderful girl who loves me for me and won't hurt me or use me then throw me away? All I want is to be happy. Is that too much to ask for? To be happy with a girl who doesn't drink, smoke, or do any drugs and will stand by my side no matter what? Is that really too much to ask for?"

This plaintive cry into the digital void, however, was swiftly undermined by the emergence of comments from a woman named Michelle Nicole Kingsbury, who asserted her status as Cyrax's girlfriend since October. Cyrax's telling silence in response to these claims only served to underscore the superficial and potentially imaginary nature of his romantic entanglements.

As we close this chapter on Cyrax's digital odyssey through 2015 and early 2016, we are left with a portrait of a man caught in a web of his own delusions. His online persona, a patchwork of grandiose ambitions and perpetual victimhood, continues to evolve and morph with each passing day. The true nature of Cyrax's reality remains as elusive as ever, obscured by the funhouse mirror of social media and his own tenuous grasp on truth. As we turn the page to the next chapter of this bizarre saga, one can only wonder what new heights of digital absurdity await.

## Chuck Steagle Saga

The year 2016 unfolds like a fever dream, with Cyrax ping-ponging between grandiose business schemes and moments of crushing self-doubt.

February saw Cyrax once again donning the ill-fitting mantle of entrepreneur. His latest venture? Peddling pottery adorned with crudely rendered 3D Celtic rune patterns. The virtual shelves of his online storefront remained dusty and untouched, a testament to the disconnect between Cyrax's inflated sense of artistic worth and the harsh realities of the marketplace. One can't help but wonder if Cyrax possessed the means or skill to actually produce these vases, should some unsuspecting soul have decided to make a purchase.

As winter gave way to spring, Cyrax's manic energy began to wane. The failure of his pottery enterprise seemed to strike a deeper chord than his previous misadventures in commerce. In a moment of uncharacteristic self-reflection, he bemoaned his inability to monetize his art. Yet, true to form, Cyrax externalized the blame, pointing an accusatory finger at nebulous "companies" for not giving him a chance.

In a twist of irony so potent it bordered on the surreal, Cyrax then pivoted to railing against those he accused of pilfering his artistic creations. This crusade against imaginary art thieves stood in stark contrast to Cyrax's own well-documented history of appropriating others' work. The baselessness of these claims became apparent as Cyrax failed to produce any evidence of stolen artwork. One can't help but speculate that this performative outrage was merely an imitation of legitimate artists' concerns, a pantomime of creativity without substance.

April ushered in a new chapter in Cyrax's musical odyssey with the launch of his record label, grandiosely titled "Metal Militia." Under this banner, he introduced the world to his band, Blackfire Lighthouse. However, the band's image - a mere screen capture from a Flash game called Punk-O-Matic - betrayed the hollowness of this latest venture. Undeterred by the lack of actual music or musicians, Cyrax forged ahead, using IMVU models to create promotional materials for his nonexistent musical outfit.

As spring bloomed, so too did Cyrax's technological ambitions. He proudly announced his foray into video game development, a claim that quickly withered under scrutiny. In reality, Cyrax had simply discovered Mugen, a fighting game engine that allows users to import pre-made character files. His grand reveal - a computer-generated bout between Fatal Fury's Joe Higashi and Bruce Lee - failed to impress his long-suffering online audience.

Faced with this latest round of indifference, Cyrax retreated into a familiar pattern of self-pity and relationship woes. In a post dripping with melodrama, he opined:

"Everyone wonders why people like me have trust issues when in a relationship. It's because when you're hurt, abused, and lied to so much, you don't know what to do, and half the time you want to end it but don't want to be the bad guy. In the end, it's not as simple as most think, especially when you truly love someone and they treat you really bad, yet you still give them everything in the hopes of them changing."

This outpouring of emotion, while seemingly heartfelt, carried with it a sinister undertone. As later events would reveal, Cyrax's portrayal of himself as the perpetual victim in romantic entanglements was a carefully crafted facade, concealing a far more troubling reality.

May brought with it a new character in the ever-expanding cast of Cyrax's digital drama: Chuck Steagle. Cyrax painted Steagle as a malevolent hacker, a digital bogeyman responsible for years of online harassment and account breaches. Little did Cyrax know that in introducing Steagle to his narrative, he was opening a Pandora's box of absurdity that would make his own eccentricities pale in comparison.

Chuck Steagle, as it turned out, was a figure of near-mythic ridiculousness in certain corners of the internet. A self-proclaimed vampire with a penchant for Conservative Christian values and public cross-dressing, Steagle was the author of the cult classic "Goth Drinking: Off While Crying." In the pantheon of internet oddities, Steagle stood as a titan of peculiarity, making him the perfect foil for Cyrax's digital misadventures.

The Cyrax-Steagle saga traced its roots back to 2013, when the pair, along with a third party named Billy Theer, attempted to form a band. Like so many of Cyrax's creative endeavors, this musical union was doomed from the start. The dissolution of this ill-fated collaboration set the stage for years of digital skulduggery and mutual accusations.

As the story goes, Steagle attempted to sabotage Cyrax's engagement to a woman named Heather by trying to set Cyrax up with another woman. When this ploy failed, Steagle allegedly sent nude photos of himself to Heather in a misguided attempt at seduction. The discovery of this betrayal led to a falling out between Cyrax and Steagle, setting the stage for years of alleged hacking and harassment.

However, like so much in Cyrax's digital realm, the truth of this narrative remained elusive. Later retellings, corroborated by Steagle himself, placed the breakdown of their friendship in 2015, citing Steagle's discovery of inappropriate messages between Cyrax and a 16-year-old as the catalyst for their rift. This version of events, however, raised more questions than it answered. How could Steagle, residing in Florida, have accessed such information about Cyrax, who lived in Ohio, without already engaging in the very hacking he was accused of?

As we peel back the layers of this digital onion, we find ourselves confronted with a disquieting possibility: that Cyrax's accusations against Steagle may have been a smokescreen, a way to deflect attention from his own questionable online behaviors. The emergence of evidence suggesting Cyrax's "proclivities toward inappropriate interactions" cast a dark shadow over his carefully constructed narrative of victimhood.

The saga of Cyrax, Steagle, and their mutual acquaintance Billy Theer reads like a fever dream of internet infamy. Theer, who met Steagle in a residential mental health program, added his own layer of peculiarity to the mix. Claiming to be a decorated military veteran with multiple tours in the Middle East, Theer's social media presence was a tapestry of outlandish claims and disturbing content.

As internet sleuths dug deeper into this triumvirate of digital eccentrics, they uncovered a web of deceit, delusion, and dark secrets. The investigation into Billy Theer's online activities led to the involvement of law enforcement, hinting at the serious nature of the content discovered.

As we close this chapter of Cyrax's ongoing saga, we're left with more questions than answers. The line between victim and perpetrator, reality and delusion, becomes increasingly blurred. Cyrax, Steagle, and

Theer emerge as unreliable narrators in their own intertwined stories, each adding layers of obfuscation to an already murky tale.

In the digital Wild West that Cyrax inhabits, truth remains an elusive commodity. As we turn the page to the next chapter of this bizarre odyssey, one can only wonder what new twists and turns await in the ever-expanding universe of Cyrax's online exploits. The saga continues, leaving us to ponder the nature of identity, truth, and reality in the age of digital self-creation.

# The Darkening Spiral

In the wake of his failed pottery enterprise, Cyrax pivoted to a new artistic medium: digital automotive design. With the zeal of a child discovering finger paints, he began churning out renderings of fantastical vehicles. The crown jewel of his vehicular visions was the "High-Powered Warmax," a creation that blurred the lines between adolescent fantasy and disturbing fixation. Cyrax meticulously detailed the Warmax's arsenal of weapons and defensive capabilities, his descriptions reading like the fevered imaginings of a Hollywood blockbuster writer crossed with a military conspiracy theorist.

The Warmax wasn't merely a flight of fancy for Cyrax; it seemed to occupy a liminal space in his mind between fiction and potential reality. This blurring of lines between the digital and the tangible would become a recurring theme in Cyrax's online saga, raising questions about his grasp on reality and the nature of his creative process.

Not content with revolutionizing imaginary warfare, Cyrax set his sights on the world of fashion. His footwear designs, unveiled with the bombast of a couturier at Paris Fashion Week, were met with a mixture of bewilderment and derision from his online audience. Undeterred by the critics, Cyrax fired back with a statement that perfectly encapsulated his defiant, if somewhat delusional, stance: "To all my haters: Sticks and stones could never shake my tone, so I'm thinking your words haven't got a hope."

This bravado, however, was short-lived. Like a pendulum swinging between grandiosity and despair, Cyrax soon retreated into his familiar persona of the lovelorn outcast. Appropriating an image of the anime character Rurouni Kenshin in a tender embrace, Cyrax penned a plaintive caption that read like a teenager's diary entry:

"This is what I want: a beautiful girl who treats me right and won't abuse or hurt me. Is that too much to ask for? Is it too much for me to ask to be happy for once in my life? So what if I don't look the best? That shouldn't matter. What should matter is how the other one is treated."

This post, dripping with self-pity and a thinly veiled plea for validation, exemplified Cyrax's ongoing struggle with self-image and relationships. The juxtaposition of his grandiose creative projects with these moments of raw vulnerability painted a portrait of a man caught between inflated self-importance and crushing insecurity.

As summer faded into autumn, Cyrax announced his latest musical venture: Urban Warfare. With the business acumen of a child running a lemonade stand, he declared that the album would be released upon receiving 25 CD pre-orders. The arbitrariness of this number and the outdated medium of CDs in an increasingly digital music landscape spoke volumes about Cyrax's disconnect from the realities of the music industry.

This disconnect became even more apparent when Cyrax launched into a multi-post tirade against the exploitative practices of record labels and the music industry at large. The irony of this rant coming from someone who had never been within spitting distance of a record contract seemed lost on Cyrax. His repeated reposting of the same diatribe, presumably due to lack of engagement, only served to underscore the echo chamber nature of his online presence.

As the year drew to a close, Cyrax's digital landscape showed signs of positive change. He claimed to have entered a new relationship and secured employment with an entity called "Miracle Riders." However, given Cyrax's penchant for blurring the lines between reality and his online personas, skepticism about these developments was warranted. The possibility that "Miracle Riders" was yet another iteration of his virtual car business loomed large.

Perhaps the most significant development of 2016 was the absence of police reports from the Cyrax household. This period of relative calm in his offline life stood in stark contrast to the tumultuous nature of his online persona, raising questions about the relationship between Cyrax's digital exploits and his real-world behavior.

As we turn the page on 2016, the saga of Cyrax continues to evolve. The coming years would bring new challenges, controversies, and digital misadventures, each adding layers to the already complex tapestry of his online existence. The line between Cyrax's virtual creations and his real-life persona would continue to blur, leaving his audience to ponder the nature of identity and reality in the digital age.

In the grand theater of internet infamy, Cyrax had secured his place as a principal player. His story, a tragicomic opera of digital delusions and real-world consequences, serves as a cautionary tale for the social media age. As we brace ourselves for the next act in this ongoing drama, one can't help but wonder: what new heights of digital absurdity await in the ever-expanding universe of Cyrax's online exploits?

# The Living Room Saga

2017 marked a year of frenzied activity for Cyrax, kicking off with a deluge of livestream videos on his Facebook account. These streams, typically filmed from Sally's living room, became known among his followers as the "Living Room Saga." This new setting served as a stage for Cyrax's increasingly erratic behavior and grandiose delusions.

January saw Cyrax convinced he had mastered the guitar, despite evidence to the contrary. His "superb production skills" made a reappearance, though the quality of his output remained questionable at best. He also began work on a music documentary and entered a new relationship, all while navigating temporary bans from livestreaming due to user reports.

February brought a new dubstep track, "Say Hello," a genre choice that demonstrated Cyrax's disconnection from current musical trends. His fashion choices during this period included wearing motorcycle glasses, which he seemed to believe gave him a "cybergoth" aesthetic. He formed a new band called "Hall Injection" and released an EP titled "Nut House."

When his musical endeavors failed to gain traction, Cyrax pivoted to offering his services as a dog sitter and babysitter. He also started selling beats for 50 cents each, launched a radio show, and even hosted a concert to "fight racism." All the while, he claimed to be working on a "video game style movie" and his first "all rap album."

Cyrax's relationship with the music industry grew increasingly strained. He made unsubstantiated claims about having a car design stolen and used in the 2017

Power Rangers film. He also alleged that a record label refused to sign him because he was "too ugly," leading to the release of a diss track called "F the Industry."

March saw Cyrax abandon an album release due to the $2 cost of official distribution. He opened an online store for "Shadow Blade" merchandise and fabricated a newsletter from the mobile game Vain Glory, claiming to be one of North America's top players. He announced a concert in Chicago, only to go on hiatus two days later.

Cyrax's relationship status fluctuated wildly. He dated a woman named Tiny, comparing their relationship to that of Naruto and Hinata, before a dramatic breakup allegedly involving Tiny's treatment of her special needs aunt. Shortly after, he claimed to be dating his "high school sweetheart," only to later mention a girlfriend named Betty.

Cyrax's creative endeavors continued to diversify, with plans for a YouTube series about zombies called "Dead Adventures" and attempts at game programming. He announced voice acting roles and new albums, though most of these projects never materialized.

As the year progressed, Cyrax's frustration with the music industry intensified. He repeatedly blamed his lack of success on his physical appearance, claiming that record labels refused to give him a chance due to his looks. This led to threats of quitting music altogether and retiring his "Shadow Blade" moniker.

Throughout 2017, Cyrax's behavior became increasingly erratic, his claims more outlandish, and his output more sporadic. The "Living Room Saga" provided his followers with a front-row seat to his digital delusions and musical misadventures, further cementing his status as an internet curiosity. As the year drew to a close, it was clear that Cyrax's journey through the digital landscape was far from over, with each new post and livestream adding another layer to his complex and often confounding online persona.

In mid-2017, Cyrax's already erratic behavior took a sharp turn towards the bizarre and concerning. The tragic passing of Linkin Park's Chester Bennington in July became a focal point for Cyrax's increasingly delusional worldview. Despite having little understanding of the circumstances surrounding Bennington's death, Cyrax didn't hesitate to speculate publicly, suggesting bullying as a cause. His misguided tribute came in the form of an announced Linkin Park mashup dubstep album, a project that, like many of his endeavors, never materialized.

Cyrax's frustration with the music industry reached a fever pitch on July 24th. In a startling video rant, he abandoned his usual self-victimization narrative for an ego-driven psychosis, declaring, "I'm going to make it in the music industry and shut you all up for good!" What's particularly notable is that this outburst occurred before Cyrax had attracted any significant attention from trolls or critics online. He was, in essence, locked in a war with himself, and losing.

The following day, Cyrax publicly contemplated retiring from music altogether. In a revealing post, he complained about his inability to maintain relationships, attributing his romantic failures to living with his mother as her caretaker. With his music career dreams fading, Cyrax pivoted to a new aspiration: becoming a professional drift racer. The only obstacle? His lack of a driver's license.

August brought a new level of fabrication to Cyrax's online presence. He spun a tale about his supposed friendship with Jason David Frank, the Green Power Ranger, claiming Frank had narrowly escaped an assassination attempt at Comic-Con. While the incident itself was verifiably true and widely reported, Cyrax's personal connection to Frank was highly dubious.

Cyrax's behavior patterns became increasingly predictable and cyclical. He would repeatedly recount his life story to elicit sympathy, announce new albums only to threaten retirement shortly after, and accuse others of hacking his accounts whenever he was caught in unseemly behavior. On August 16th, for instance, he accused his ex-girlfriend Tiffany of hacking his account to make it appear he was cheating on his current girlfriend, Abby.

A strange police report from August 20th added another layer of confusion to Cyrax's narrative. One of his neighbors called for a welfare check after Chance's "ex-boyfriend" allegedly threatened Sally over the phone. The ambiguity surrounding this incident only added to the growing tapestry of Cyrax's convoluted personal life.

As summer turned to fall, Cyrax's online activities became increasingly desperate and dishonest. He began using a rap battle app to release what he claimed were his own songs. He continued to blame "lookism" in the music industry for his lack of success, now including promoters in his list of culprits.

Cyrax's romantic life remained a source of drama and deception. While still ostensibly in a relationship with Abby, he began posting as if he were single, likely using Facebook's privacy settings to hide these posts from her. He even organized a meet-and-greet event in Akron for his "fan base," though reports suggest he failed to show up for his own gathering.

Perhaps most egregiously, Cyrax began selling digitally traced and filtered stock images as his own original artwork. When called out on this deception, he would often accuse others of stealing his work, a tactic that became increasingly transparent over time. His art "sales" ranged from traced fan art to famous photographs of celebrities like Audrey Hepburn, which he attempted to sell for $40.

Throughout this period, Cyrax's behavior became a study in digital desperation. Each post, each new scheme, each fabricated story seemed designed to attract attention, sympathy, or admiration. Yet, ironically, it was this very behavior that would eventually attract the kind of attention Cyrax seemed ill-equipped to handle

## Cyrax's Late 2017 Spiral

As autumn 2017 approached, Cyrax's online behavior became increasingly erratic and disconnected from reality. On September 12th, he held a memorial not for 9/11, but for "911" - September 1st, 2001. This misguided tribute featured images of a car he designed in a drifting game, adorned with an American flag and "911" on the hood, likely misinterpreting an in-game police car designation.

Throughout September and October, Cyrax cycled through his now-familiar pattern of threatening retirement, complaining about the music industry, and fabricating interactions with major record labels. He claimed to have received an email from Warner Brothers Records' A&R department rejecting him based on his looks, a story that bore all the hallmarks of his typical fabrications.

Cyrax's romantic life remained turbulent. He began a relationship with a woman named Maria before officially ending things with his previous girlfriend, Abby. His post about the breakup with Abby revealed potential issues with her parents' disapproval, likely stemming from his public posts about other relationships.

A revealing comment thread on one of Cyrax's posts about Social Security benefits hinted at deeper issues. It suggested that a female acquaintance, possibly Abby, was at risk of losing her Supplemental Security Income and facing potential homelessness. This experience seemed to influence Cyrax's self-perception, as he began referring to himself as a "special needs artist" and considered making a YouTube documentary series about his experiences.

As October progressed, Cyrax's creative output became increasingly scattered. He published poems about PTSD and samurai, many of which appeared to be plagiarized.

He claimed success as an author despite no evidence of published works. He briefly pivoted to "professional photography" and then to creating "micro pottery" - tiny vases he claimed to have sculpted and painted by hand but were clearly 3D renders.

Cyrax's frustration with his perceived lack of success manifested in increasingly angry posts. He complained about others having it easy while he struggled, despite living rent-free and spending his days making music. In a moment of poetic irony, he followed this complaint with a post boasting about his skills at playing GameCube.

The nadir of this period came when Cyrax reacted explosively to constructive criticism from a commenter named Hunter. Hunter's suggestion that Cyrax should ignore his detractors and focus on self-improvement triggered a series of lengthy, repetitive live streams. In these streams, Cyrax rehashed his life story, emphasizing his medical challenges at birth and claiming a unique understanding of facing death daily.

These streams, some lasting nearly an hour, demonstrated Cyrax's hypersensitivity to criticism and his tendency to use his medical history as a shield against any form of accountability. His repetitive, self-aggrandizing monologues revealed a deeply insecure individual struggling to cope with the realities of his life and the criticisms he faced online.

As 2017 drew to a close, Cyrax's online presence had devolved into a cycle of grandiose claims, fabricated successes, and explosive reactions to even the mildest criticism. His behavior during this period set the stage for increased attention from online trolls, as his hypersensitivity and tendency to overreact made him an easy target for provocation.

## The Delusions Deepen: Cyrax's Descent into Fantasy

As 2017 drew to a close and 2018 began, Cyrax's online behavior continued its downward spiral into an increasingly bizarre and disconnected reality. His penchant for exaggeration and outright fabrication reached new heights, exemplified by his claim of losing "a shot at the prize of $125 million" in an online poker tournament - a sum far beyond any realistic online poker prize pool.

Cyrax's musical aspirations took on a new form as he rebranded himself as "Virus" and claimed co-founder status of a record label called Bloodshot Records. This venture seemed to be little more than a vehicle for his own musical output and a misguided attempt to sign as many artists as possible, demonstrating a fundamental misunderstanding of how record labels operate.

His tendency to revisit and reframe past conflicts was evident in his renewed focus on the Eric Scrubble and Killer Clown Sounds drama. Cyrax conveniently rewrote history, claiming he was owed money and had been mistreated, while glossing over the fact that he had been kicked out of the label for theft.

Cyrax's disconnect from reality extended beyond the music industry. He railed against book publishers for requesting payment to publish his work, seemingly unaware of the standard practices in the publishing industry. His naivety was further highlighted by his belief in a supposed offer from Tech N9ne's Strange Music label for a $1 million contract for his beats - an offer that was almost certainly a fabrication or a cruel prank.

In a moment of vulnerability, Cyrax shared a post about playing online games with long-time friends at 4 AM, offering a glimpse into the loneliness and social isolation that seemed to fuel much of his online behavior. However, any empathy this might have engendered was quickly overshadowed by his continued problematic behavior.

Cyrax's grandiose claims extended into the tech world, with him announcing plans to create a social network combining elements of Facebook and MySpace. This declaration, made without irony on Facebook itself, demonstrated his complete lack of understanding of the complexities involved in such an endeavor.

His forays into professional gaming were equally delusional, with Cyrax claiming he should be paid for his skills in Call of Duty: Black Ops, despite no evidence of exceptional ability.

A visit to the doctor revealed that Cyrax had shrunk an inch in height, from 5'3" to 5'2" - a physical diminishment that seemed to mirror his shrinking grasp on reality.

When faced with honest criticism of his music, Cyrax's response was characteristically defensive and lacking in self-awareness. A livestream intended to rebut his critic instead highlighted his inability to handle constructive feedback. For once, Cyrax seemed genuinely shaken by the words of his detractor, particularly when confronted with the reality of someone balancing a full-time job, family, and a more successful musical career than his own.

However, true to form, Cyrax's goldfish-like attention span soon led him back to his racing games, where he continued to blur the lines between virtual and reality by presenting his in-game car designs as if they were real-world achievements. His attempt to sell these virtual designs to an actual art publishing company was met with predictable dismissal, further highlighting the growing chasm between Cyrax's perception of his talents and the harsh realities of the creative industries he sought to conquer.

As 2018 progressed, it became increasingly clear that Cyrax was trapped in a cycle of delusion and disappointment, unable or unwilling to confront the realities of his situation or to make meaningful changes to his approach to life and art. His online presence continued to be a source of fascination and frustration for observers, a digital train wreck that was as compelling as it was concerning.

## The D pics – The Road to Lolcow

As 2018 progressed, Chance "Cyrax" Wilkins found himself on an unexpected path to internet notoriety. While his dreams of musical stardom remained as distant as ever, his incessant Facebook posting and inflammatory responses to criticism began to attract increasing engagement. Unbeknownst to Cyrax, he was taking his first steps towards becoming what internet culture refers to as a "lolcow" - a person who, through their actions and reactions online, becomes a source of entertainment and mockery for others.

Cyrax's artistic endeavors took a new turn as he joined DeviantArt, attempting to sell his "art pieces" for $1 each. These pieces were little more than photos with filters applied, demonstrating his continued disconnect between his perceived and actual artistic abilities. His musical output continued unabated, with the release of an album titled "Blackout," featuring a hue-shifted image of Master Chief from Halo as its cover art - a choice that perfectly encapsulated Cyrax's disregard for copyright and lack of originality.

His streaming privileges on Facebook were temporarily revoked, allegedly due to a harmonica cover of a Linkin Park song. This setback did little to temper Cyrax's delusions about the music industry. He invented a bizarre narrative about record labels and studios from the 1950s helping artists for free, using this fabricated history to criticize modern labels for not doing the same for him. He applied this same flawed logic to book publishers, searching in vain for a company that would publish his works - including a purported high school manga based on his life - for free.

March saw a brief reconciliation between Cyrax and his former associate Eric Scruballo, leading to an opportunity to perform at a live venue in June. However, this relationship, like many in Cyrax's life, was short-lived and headed towards self-destruction due to Cyrax's continued misunderstanding of basic business principles.

A significant turning point came in May when Cyrax fell victim to a catfishing scheme. An individual named Lewis, posing as a female admirer, manipulated Cyrax into sharing intimate images. These images were then used to blackmail Cyrax, though the exact nature of Lewis's demands remains unclear. In a characteristic move, Cyrax attempted to save face by claiming his account had been hacked, a lie he would resort to repeatedly in the future when faced with similar situations.

This incident marked the beginning of a pattern that would come to define Cyrax's online presence: a cycle of poor decision-making, victimization, and subsequent attempts at deception to preserve his image. His inability to learn from these experiences, coupled with his continued provocative behavior online, set the stage for increasingly fraught interactions with his growing audience of critics and trolls.

As 2018 wore on, it became clear that Cyrax was trapped in a web of his own making. His desperate attempts at fame, his willingness to believe in obviously false promises, and his inability to handle criticism were creating a perfect storm of internet notoriety. While he may have dreamed of becoming famous for his music or art, Cyrax was instead becoming infamous for his online antics and his seemingly endless capacity for self-delusion.

The stage was set for Cyrax's transformation from a struggling, delusional artist into a full-fledged internet phenomenon - a transformation that would bring him the attention he craved, but in ways he could never have anticipated or desired.

## Delusions of Grandeur: Cyrax's Summer of Discontent

June 2018 marked a new chapter in Cyrax's ongoing saga of self-delusion and digital drama. The month began with a literal pain in his foot - an infected toe that Cyrax dramatically framed as a "fight for his life." This minor medical issue did little to dampen his inflated sense of self-importance, as he quickly pivoted to boasting about his supposed desirability among women, claiming that his non-existent wealth and fame were attracting admirers.

The cancellation of Cyrax's much-anticipated live concert was a significant blow, though the reasons he provided - people "not getting the dates right" - seemed suspiciously vague. This setback, however, only fueled his creative output, resulting in an ill-conceived diss track aimed at then-President Donald Trump and the creation of a new YouTube channel called "Gamer Zone." True to form, even this new venture was marred by controversy, with at least one of the channel's logos blatantly stolen from an existing rap battle channel.

Cyrax's disconnect from financial reality reached new heights when he announced plans to reveal the secrets of achieving musical success without spending money. His "great tips" amounted to little more than a list of free music-making apps, with no concrete advice on how to monetize one's efforts. This misguided attempt at mentorship highlighted the vast chasm between Cyrax's perception of his success and the harsh realities of his situation.

The fragile reconciliation with Eric Scruballo crumbled once again, leading to a public spat that exposed the depths of Cyrax's delusions. In a video response to Eric's criticisms, Cyrax made outlandish claims about being "Renation's number one artist from 2010 up to this year" and insisted he was "making money." His attempt to showcase his supposed wealth fell flat when he abruptly decided not to "waste that on you," a transparent cover for the fact that there was likely no money to display.

Cyrax's physical appearance became another point of contention when he shared images of his supposed "chiseled abs and pecs," adorned with what appeared to be a discount Sonichu necklace. This bizarre fusion of self-aggrandizement and pop culture appropriation drew parallels to other infamous internet personalities, suggesting a shared pathology among those who find themselves at the center of online ridicule.

Throughout this period, Cyrax's behavior continued to follow a predictable pattern: grandiose claims of success and popularity, followed by flimsy attempts to prove his worth, all underpinned by a fundamental misunderstanding of how the music industry - and indeed, the world at large - operates. His ability to twist any situation, no matter how negative, into a narrative of personal triumph spoke to a deep-seated need for validation and recognition.

As the summer of 2018 progressed, it became increasingly clear that Cyrax was trapped in a cycle of his own making. Each setback was reframed as a victory, each criticism as jealousy, and each failed venture as a stepping stone to inevitable success. This pattern of behavior not only alienated potential allies in the music industry but also made Cyrax an irresistible target for online trolls and critics.

The juxtaposition of Cyrax's grandiose self-image with the reality of his situation created a perfect storm of internet notoriety. His journey from aspiring musician to digital pariah was accelerating, fueled by his own delusions and the relentless scrutiny of an online audience that found his antics both fascinating and appalling.

As the summer of 2018 progressed, Cyrax's grandiose self-image continued to expand beyond the realm of music into new creative territories. On June 26th, he ventured into filmmaking, posting an unofficial trailer for a movie titled "Lady in White." The production quality of this trailer was characteristically poor, serving more as a testament to Cyrax's delusions of grandeur than any actual filmmaking ability.

In a bizarre attempt to associate himself with genuine celebrity, Cyrax doctored an image of a Google Hangouts session featuring the late Chester Bennington, crudely inserting his own face to create the illusion of a personal connection with the Linkin Park frontman. This manipulated image perfectly encapsulated Cyrax's desperate need for validation and recognition from the music industry he so admired.

July 4th saw Cyrax celebrating independence day by announcing yet another relationship and releasing a new track called "Please Notice Me." In keeping with his pattern of fabricating success, he claimed this track was a "number one hit" before it was even published. His lies extended beyond music, with Cyrax claiming to have turned down a deal with Hoonigan, a popular racing channel, due to insufficient YouTube subscribers. He later admitted to not even having a driver's license, exposing the hollowness of his racing aspirations.

Cyrax's attention-seeking behavior took a darker turn as he fabricated a story about doctors warning him to stop making music or risk losing his voice. This led to a series of pity-baiting posts, retelling his life story for the umpteenth time, each iteration more extreme than the last. He briefly pivoted to photography before announcing yet another relationship, this time rekindling things with his ex-girlfriend Abby.

August was relatively quiet, marked by Cyrax mourning a former bandmate who allegedly overdosed on heroin and meth simultaneously. His hypocrisy was on full display as he railed against art theft, only to have his own "artwork" suffer copyright takedowns for being stolen images from Google.

Financial reality hit hard when Cyrax's much-anticipated music royalties amounted to a mere $14, a sum he struggled to claim from the distribution platform. This disappointment led to public rants against the platform on Facebook.

September saw Cyrax branching out into horror films, with a trailer for "The Darkness" in which he played all the characters himself, reminiscent of Eddie

Murphy's multiple roles in "Norbit." This foray into filmmaking seemed to be yet another attempt to diversify his perceived talents and achieve the fame that continued to elude him in the music world.

Throughout this period, early signs of troll activity began to emerge. Individuals online started impersonating Cyrax, a tactic that proved effective in provoking reactions from him. This marked the beginning of a new phase in Cyrax's online presence, one where he would increasingly find himself the target of deliberate provocations and mockery.

As fall approached, Cyrax's online persona had evolved into a complex tapestry of delusions, spanning music, film, racing, and beyond. Each new venture seemed to be an attempt to reinvent himself and achieve the recognition he so desperately craved. However, his consistent pattern of exaggeration, fabrication, and poor execution only served to further cement his status as an object of fascination and ridicule in the online world.

The months ahead promised to bring new challenges for Cyrax, as the attention he had long sought began to manifest in ways he could neither control nor fully comprehend.

September 2018 marked a pivotal moment in Cyrax's online saga with the release of one of his most memorable videos: a dance battle response to an old rival. This bizarre performance, described by observers as "amazing, excellent, divine, beautiful," exemplified Cyrax's unique blend of misplaced confidence and unintentional comedy.

Under the moniker of Darkar Films, his fantasy production company, Cyrax rehashed his tutorial on becoming a successful artist without spending money. This latest iteration, like its predecessors, offered little in the way of practical advice but provided ample insight into Cyrax's delusional mindset.

October, fittingly the "spooky month," saw the release of Cyrax's magnum opus: "The Darkness." This incomprehensible short film began with Cyrax entering his house, followed by a series of disjointed scenes featuring PewDiePie-style face cams, static-filled radio stations, and inexplicable mumbling. The plot, if one could call it that, involved Cyrax wandering aimlessly, becoming hypnotized by a forest, and being haunted by voice lines from the baby character in "Five Nights at Freddy's: Sister Location" - a clear copyright infringement that Cyrax seemed oblivious to.

The film's climax, if it can be called such, featured Cyrax choking to death, followed by someone else's creepy horror video and several minutes of darkness. Despite - or perhaps because of - its incoherence, "The Darkness" garnered more views than

Cyrax's usual content, inadvertently setting the stage for his rise to internet infamy.

October 19th is marked in the "official Cyrax timeline" as the day his nemesis, Music Biz Marty, discovered his existence. This introduction, facilitated by someone known as "the boy blue," occurred while Marty was harassing one of Cyrax's ex-girlfriends, Candle. While the exact timeline is disputed, Facebook activity suggests that Cyrax entered a relationship with Candle on October 11th, which lasted until late November.

During this relationship, Cyrax's online activity noticeably decreased, possibly due to the stabilizing influence of having a girlfriend. He even went so far as to post about his prospects of marrying Candle and selecting godparents for their future children - plans that, fortunately, never materialized.

The relative quiet of November 2018 would prove to be the calm before the storm.

Unbeknownst to Cyrax, the attention garnered by "The Darkness" and his other online antics was about to catapult him into a new level of internet notoriety. The discovery of his content by Music Biz Marty would set in motion a chain of events that would expose Cyrax's more problematic behaviors and propel him further into the spotlight of online ridicule.

As 2018 drew to a close, Cyrax stood on the precipice of a new chapter in his digital saga. His delusional pursuits of fame through music, film, and social media had laid the groundwork for what was to come. The combination of his grandiose self-image, his willingness to overshare personal information, and his tendency to react dramatically to provocation made him an ideal target for the darker corners of internet culture.

The months ahead would see Cyrax's online presence evolve from a source of bemused entertainment to a cautionary tale of internet infamy. His journey from aspiring artist to digital pariah was about to accelerate, driven by forces beyond his control and fueled by his own inability to step away from the digital spotlight he so desperately craved.

# Wrapping up 2018

December 2018 kicked off with a bang in Cyrax's online world. He launched a livestream that would go down in his personal history - a desperate plea for help that mixed drama, delusion, and a dash of digital panhandling.

Cyrax called on his small following to chip in and save his supposed girlfriend, Candle, from her life in Mississippi. He spun a tale of woe: Candle was disabled, half-blind, and supposedly abused by parents who stole her disability checks and left her homeless. It was a story designed to tug at heartstrings and open wallets.

But reality had other plans. Within a day, Candle herself popped up online with a comment that blew Cyrax's story apart: "Why would I come to you after the way you did me?" Just like that, Cyrax's rescue mission crumbled.

True to form, Cyrax's response was swift and predictable. He blocked Candle and turned to Facebook to bemoan his bad luck in love. "How do I always end up with all these girls who are not right in the head?" he asked, seemingly blind to his own role in these romantic disasters.

As Christmas approached, Cyrax tried to keep up his usual online act. He bragged about non-existent fans and made-up victories in professional drift racing. It was as if he thought he could will his fantasies into reality through sheer online persistence.

But the Candle situation wasn't done haunting him. She released a video titled "Chance Wilkins is Insane." While the video itself was private, its mere existence sent Cyrax into a spiral. He posted a tearful message claiming to be the victim of Candle's harassment and lies, frustrated that even the police wouldn't step in to help him.

The drama took a darker turn when Eric Scruballo, a familiar name in Cyrax's world, claimed that Candle had shared Cyrax's real address online, potentially opening the door to real-world harassment.

This whole episode showcased the typical elements of Cyrax's online life: oversharing, exaggeration, rocky relationships, and a quick retreat to playing the victim when things go south. It also highlighted how his online actions were starting to have real-world consequences.

As 2018 came to a close, the Candle saga set the stage for more drama to come. Cyrax's habit of airing his personal life online, combined with his growing notoriety, made him an easy target for internet troublemakers. The months ahead would see Cyrax dealing not just with fallout from failed relationships, but also with the growing impact of his expanding online presence on his real life.

# The Candle Inferno

As the clock struck midnight on January 1, 2019, Chance "Cyrax" Wilkins found himself not in celebratory revelry, but under the scrutiny of local law enforcement. A welfare check, its details shrouded in bureaucratic redaction, marked the ominous beginning of what would prove to be a year of unprecedented turmoil in the online saga of Akron's most infamous aspiring musician.

The specter of Candle, Cyrax's recent ex-girlfriend and newfound digital nemesis, loomed large over this New Year's intervention. On the surface, Cyrax's initial Facebook post exuded relief, a digital sigh proclaiming victory over Candle's alleged campaign of harassment. "I want to say thank you to everyone," he wrote, basking in the illusory glow of communal triumph, "because of all of you, Candle has been stopped and her posts and videos removed."

But beneath this veneer of resolution lay a web of deception and digital skulduggery that would soon unravel in spectacular fashion. Unbeknownst to his loyal Facebook following, Cyrax had brokered a Faustian pact with Candle - a mutual agreement of digital silence, each vowing to erase the other from their online existence. Yet, in a move that would prove characteristic of his inability to let sleeping dogs lie, Cyrax couldn't resist the siren call of social media martyrdom.

Employing what he doubtless considered a masterful stratagem, Cyrax continued to post about Candle while adjusting his privacy settings to exclude her from his digital diatribes. But Candle, proving more adept at the art of online warfare than her ex-flame, had anticipated this betrayal. Armed with an alternate Facebook account, she lay in wait, monitoring Cyrax's every digital move.

The inevitable revelation of Cyrax's duplicity came swiftly and without mercy. "Haha, still here," Candle's mocking comment appeared beneath one of Cyrax's clandestine posts, "Not all the posts are taken down. He broke the deal." With these words, the fragile peace between the former lovers shattered, igniting a conflagration of mutual recrimination that would engulf Cyrax's online world for weeks to come.

Cyrax, his digital ego bruised and battered, retaliated with a fury born of desperation and delusion. He shared a video of Candle accusing him of obsession, appending a call to arms that would make any responsible social media user recoil: "I give everyone full permission to go all out on this." The comment section beneath this inflammatory post quickly devolved into a digital gladiatorial arena, with Candle gleefully offering to share audio evidence of Cyrax's threatening behavior.

Indeed, a recording soon surfaced of Cyrax's voice, dripping with misplaced bravado and thinly veiled threats: "So you want to keep playing that game? I can't will have you arrested for harassment. So guess what? I ain't the one going to jail. The one that's going to jail is you. So keep running your mouth, you little bitch. Guarantee you're going to go to jail."

As January wore on, Cyrax's obsession with Candle seemed to grow exponentially. Each day brought new posts, each more desperate and self-pitying than the last. On January 7th, he cast himself as the ultimate victim, claiming Candle had "mentally and verbally abused him and traumatized him worse than any of his other exes." Two days later, another post prompted Candle to create a video addressing Cyrax directly, a digital manifesto that remains preserved on YouTube to this day.

"Yo, this is your girl Rebecca," Candle begins, her voice a mixture of exasperation and disdain. "This is a video to prove how bad of a stalker Chance is. He sat there and found out where I live. Not creepy at all, not a stalker vibe at all. You're so stupid, kid. Leave me alone. I don't like you, never liked you. I was nice to you 'cuz I felt bad for you, and then I found out you're a liar. You're just butthurt 'cuz I won't date you. Stop harassing me, you nutcase."

The uncanny similarities between Candle and Cyrax's speech patterns led some online sleuths to speculate that Candle might be a troll, a digital provocateur playing an elaborate game. Yet, the raw emotion evident in her videos and posts suggested a genuine, if dysfunctional, conflict between two deeply troubled individuals.

As the digital war raged on, Cyrax's tactics grew increasingly desperate. He instructed his followers to block Candle, to report her videos, to silence her by any means necessary. In a final, grandiose gesture of self-delusion, he claimed that Candle's actions threatened a potentially life-changing deal with "Reborn Records," a supposedly major nonprofit label that had shown interest in his work.

"This isn't just a little issue," Cyrax proclaimed, his digital voice quavering with desperation, "this is huge, and she needs to be stopped ASAP." But to those who had long observed Cyrax's online behavior, this latest claim rang hollow - just another convenient excuse for a man who seemed pathologically incapable of walking away from conflict, no matter how petty or self-destructive.

# The Reborn Records Reckoning: Cyrax's Collision with Reality

As January 2019 unfolded, Chance "Cyrax" Wilkins found himself embroiled in a confrontation that would lay bare the vast chasm between his delusional self-perception and the harsh realities of the music industry. This pivotal moment came in the form of an email from a representative of Reborn Records, a missive that would serve as both a mirror and a hammer to Cyrax's fragile ego.

The email, penned with a level of patience and kindness rarely seen in the cutthroat world of music production, attempted to gently guide Cyrax towards an understanding of his shortcomings. "The issue is that your demos all use loops," the representative explained, his words a masterclass in constructive criticism. He went on to elucidate the importance of original composition, drawing analogies to sports recruitment to illustrate the competitive nature of the industry.

"We are not an education group, a school, or a charity," the email continued, each word a nail in the coffin of Cyrax's musical aspirations. "We are a record label that pays people upfront for quality beats. We want top-quality musicians who make their own stuff, not rip it, not loop it, just create."

In a twist of irony that would not be lost on Cyrax's growing cadre of online observers, the representative's claim that they were "not a charity" would prove to be the most charitable act Cyrax had yet encountered in his quixotic quest for musical fame. The email concluded with a note of encouragement that would prove tragically misplaced: "I think you're a good dude."

Cyrax's response to this thoughtful critique was as predictable as it was disheartening. In a Facebook post dripping with indignation, he shared the email, proclaiming, "This is the kind of shit that pisses me off. They act all interested and once I explain my situation, they pull this and kindly tell me to fuck off."

The digital peanut gallery, however, was not on Cyrax's side. His followers, in a rare moment of clarity, sided with the Reborn Records representative, praising the email's well-constructed arguments and the extraordinary effort taken to inform Cyrax of his shortcomings. Yet, even in the face of this unanimous verdict, Cyrax remained steadfast in his delusions, linking to a since-deleted rant video that presumably rehashed his usual litany of excuses.

The situation escalated when the Reborn Records representative, upon discovering Cyrax's public tantrum, fired off a second email. This missive, tinged with frustration, cut to the heart of Cyrax's fundamental misunderstanding of the music industry: "Seriously man, I was trying to help you, but instead of facing up to a challenge, you just think everyone is against you... Stay humble, learn the tools, and maybe you'll get a shot. But going around thinking we owe you something for nothing? Dude, we're a record label, not a charity."

Cyrax's response to this second email was to double down on his victim narrative, sharing it on Facebook with the caption: "This just proves even more how messed up record labels can be these days. SMH. What happened to the days where labels used to actually care about the artist and not the money?" In his haste to paint himself as the wronged party, Cyrax inadvertently revealed more than he intended - an open tab for an adult website visible in his screenshot, a detail his followers were quick to point out.

As his followers once again sided with the Reborn Records representative, Cyrax's arguments grew increasingly desperate and contradictory. He claimed the label had approached him (a demonstrable falsehood), insisted he couldn't create original music due to only owning a Chromebook (despite evidence to the contrary), and even went so far as to claim Reborn Records was "fake" because they had checked his personal page.

In a video response that was painful to watch, Cyrax, visibly dehydrated and struggling to articulate his thoughts, attempted to discredit Reborn Records while promoting his own label, Bloodshot. The irony of boasting about his label's ability to help artists make money, when he himself was penniless, seemed lost on him.

## Shadows of the Past: Cyrax's Carceral Confession

As the Reborn Records debacle unfolded, a darker aspect of Cyrax's past emerged from the shadows, casting a pall over his already tarnished online persona. In a rare moment of candor, Cyrax acknowledged a fact long buried in his digital narrative: his incarceration in 2012. This admission, however, was not offered as a moment of honest self-reflection, but rather as yet another excuse in his ever-growing arsenal of justifications for his current circumstances.

"I went back to jail in 2012," Cyrax confessed, his words dripping with self-pity rather than remorse. This statement, dropped casually into one of his rambling diatribes, was presented as an explanation for his chronic unemployment. Yet, in true Cyrax fashion, this admission was only a partial truth, a carefully curated snippet of his troubled past designed to elicit sympathy while obscuring the more damning details of his actions.

What Cyrax conveniently omitted from this narrative was the reason for his incarceration - a violent altercation with his elderly adoptive mother, Sally. The incident, which had occurred years earlier, involved Cyrax attempting to choke the very woman who had taken him in and raised him. This act of domestic violence, a chilling indicator of Cyrax's capacity for harm, was conspicuously absent from his retelling.

The juxtaposition of Cyrax's partial admission and glaring omission painted a troubling picture of a man incapable of genuine introspection or accountability. His willingness to use his time in jail as an excuse for his current failures, while simultaneously refusing to acknowledge the gravity of his actions or express remorse, spoke volumes about his character.

This revelation added a new layer of complexity to the Cyrax saga. It raised questions about the extent of his past misdeeds and the potential for future transgressions. For his online followers, it cast his endless complaints and excuses in a new, more sinister light. Was Cyrax merely a hapless, delusional aspiring musician, or was there a more dangerous individual lurking beneath the surface of his digital persona?

The jail admission also provided context for some of Cyrax's more erratic behaviors. His claims of sleeping only five hours a week, while likely an exaggeration, hinted at potential mental health issues that may have been exacerbated by his time in incarceration. The sleep deprivation he boasted about, if true, could explain some of his more outlandish actions and beliefs, as such extreme fatigue is known to induce hallucinations and impair cognitive function.

Cyrax's brief acknowledgment of his criminal past added yet another layer to his complex and troubling online presence. It served as a stark reminder that behind the digital drama and musical aspirations lay a real person with a history of violence and legal troubles. This revelation would undoubtedly color future interactions with Cyrax, as his followers and detractors alike grappled with the implications of this new information.

The coming months would see Cyrax continue to navigate the treacherous waters of internet fame, his past misdeeds now an inescapable part of his narrative. Whether this admission would lead to genuine introspection and change, or simply become another tool in Cyrax's arsenal of excuses, remained to be seen. One thing was certain: the saga of Chance "Cyrax" Wilkins had taken a darker turn, one that would have far-reaching consequences for his online persona and real-world interactions.

While January 2019 continued its relentless march, Chance "Cyrax" Wilkins found himself embroiled in an ever-deepening quagmire of his own making. The brief respite offered by his interactions with Reborn Records was abruptly shattered by the resurgence of his digital nemesis, Candle. Like a specter from his recent past, she emerged with threats that sent shockwaves through Cyrax's already precarious world.

Candle's claim was as simple as it was devastating: she possessed video evidence of Cyrax attempting to blackmail her. While the veracity of this claim remained unverified, the palpable fear it instilled in Cyrax suggested there might be more than a kernel of truth to her allegations. The threat of legal repercussions loomed large, casting a shadow over Cyrax's digital domain.

In a move that perfectly encapsulated his approach to life's challenges, Cyrax's response to this potential legal threat was to literally hide. "I hid until the police left," he later boasted, seemingly oblivious to how this admission painted him not as a clever evader of justice, but as a man-child ducking responsibility. In the same breath, he called out for Sally, the very woman he had once physically assaulted, in a moment of crisis - a jarring juxtaposition that highlighted the complex and often troubling dynamics of his home life.

True to form, Cyrax swiftly transmuted this brush with the law into yet another excuse for his lack of success in the music industry. In his mind, it wasn't his lack of talent or originality holding him back, but rather these external forces conspiring against him. This narrative of perpetual victimhood had become Cyrax's calling card, a well-worn path he trod with increasing frequency.

However, the digital world waits for no man, and Cyrax was soon back to his relentless pursuit of internet fame and fortune. His latest scheme? Positioning himself as a "professional YouTube channel intro maker." This grandiose title belied the reality of his methods - using simple, freely available software that "an 8-year-old can operate" to create generic intros. In a move that perfectly encapsulated his lack of originality, he christened his new venture "Nuclear Reactor," a name he had already used for a reaction channel.

But it was Cyrax's casual use of racial slurs that would prove to be the match that ignited the powder keg of his online community. When confronted about his liberal use of the n-word, Cyrax's immediate response was to claim victimhood once again. He made a desperate post attempting to defend his actions, but found himself in the unfamiliar position of having none of his friends rally to his side.

Faced with this unprecedented wave of criticism from his own digital allies, Cyrax retreated to his most basic defense mechanism: wholesale blocking of dissenters. Under the flimsy pretense of purging his account of "Candle's minions," he began a digital purge of anyone who dared to express disagreement with his actions or views.

This period marked a significant turning point in Cyrax's online saga. The veneer of the misunderstood artist he had so carefully cultivated was beginning to crack, revealing glimpses of a more troubling personality beneath. His casual racism, his attempts at blackmail, his evasion of law enforcement - all of these elements combined to paint a picture of a man not merely deluded about his talents, but potentially dangerous in his desperation for fame and validation.

# Cyrax's February Fury

As the calendar flipped to February 2019, Chance "Cyrax" Wilkins found himself spiraling further into a vortex of digital drama and real-world consequences. The month began ominously, with Sally, his long-suffering adoptive mother, once again forced to summon law enforcement to their shared domicile. This time, the catalyst was a series of online threats directed at Cyrax, presumably from his digital nemesis, Candle. The incident served as a stark reminder of the increasingly blurred lines between Cyrax's online persona and his offline reality.

On the sixth day of the month, Cyrax took to his digital pulpit to rail against those he perceived as undervaluing his musical offerings. His diatribe, a masterclass in cognitive dissonance, revealed the depths of his delusions about his place in the music industry:

"You know what confuses me? All these artists say they want beats from me, and they're all willing to pay $10 for 10 solid beats to own flat out. Then when the time comes, they turn tail, back out, and run off like WTF. And y'all wonder why I can't make it as a producer. That's the reason, 'cuz too many mofos want to play games and try and take advantage of me."

This tirade, dripping with self-pity and misplaced indignation, inadvertently exposed the glaring disconnect between Cyrax's perception of his worth and the market's valuation of his work. His offer of ten beats for a mere ten dollars spoke volumes about the quality of his output, yet in his mind, it was the potential buyers who were at fault for not recognizing his genius.

In a moment of unintentional honesty, Cyrax's post seemed to acknowledge the criticism leveled at him by Reborn Records. He admitted that his beats were "loop style," a far cry from his previous claims of original composition. However, rather than recognizing this as a limitation, Cyrax attempted to frame it as a deliberate artistic choice, one that mainstream artists simply failed to appreciate:

"They don't respect music anymore and how simple but dope at Loop style beats like I do evolved into what they are now. It's sad to say, but half you mainstream guys need to learn and do your music history and take a look at where music started with guys like Beethoven."

The invocation of Beethoven in defense of his use of pre-made loops was a cognitive leap that left even Cyrax's most ardent supporters scratching their heads. It was a perfect encapsulation of his tendency to grasp at any justification, no matter how tenuous, to avoid confronting his own shortcomings.

The constant barrage of criticism and trolling in his YouTube comment sections began to take its toll. In a move that had become almost routine, Cyrax announced his retirement from music. This declaration, like so many before it, was less a genuine decision to step away from his craft and more a cry for attention and validation.

But as the month wore on, a more sinister turn of events loomed on the horizon. The constant online harassment, the legal threats, the familial strife - all of these factors were coalescing into a perfect storm of stress and instability for Cyrax. His online behavior, always erratic, began to take on a darker, more desperate tone.

The stage was set for a dramatic escalation in the tragic comedy that was Cyrax's life.

# Fred and The Tree Incident

On the night of February 25th, in an incident that seemed lifted from the pages of a gothic novel, a tree in the neighboring area toppled perilously close to Cyrax's residence. True to form, Cyrax wasted no time in spinning this natural occurrence into a narrative of personal peril, dramatically proclaiming how the falling timber could have easily claimed his life.

This brush with arboreal danger marked the beginning of a period of escalating tension in Cyrax's world. The following weeks saw a series of mostly redacted police reports emanating from his domicile, hinting at troubles brewing beneath the surface of his digital facade.

By mid-March, the relative calm was shattered by the reemergence of Candle,

Cyrax's digital nemesis. Her return heralded a new wave of accusations, more scathing and disturbing than ever before. In a live video broadcast on Facebook, Candle unleashed a torrent of allegations that painted Cyrax in a truly sinister light:

"All you mothers out there that have young children, be warned of this guy named Chance Wilkins," Candle began, her voice trembling with a mix of anger and urgency. "He'll jack off on your children. Not only that, he'll sit there and jack off on video chat with them. He'll sit there and threaten to kill your children if they don't sleep with him."

These accusations, while unsubstantiated, were deeply troubling. They suggested a level of depravity that went far beyond Cyrax's usual online antics. While concrete evidence was lacking, the gravity of these claims was enough to sway even some of Cyrax's closest allies. Becky, who had once been concerned enough to call in a welfare check on Cyrax, and Abby, with whom Cyrax had rekindled a relationship in April, both distanced themselves from him in light of the information Candle shared.

Candle's crusade against Cyrax took on an almost vigilante quality. She initiated multiple welfare checks on Cyrax's residence, seemingly in an attempt to keep him in check through the looming presence of law enforcement. In one recorded call, she expressed concern about Cyrax's mental state and potential danger to himself and others.

The situation took another bizarre turn when rumors began to circulate that Candle had taken her own life. Cyrax found himself the target of blame for her supposed passing, adding another layer of stress to his already precarious mental state. The fact that these rumors later proved false did little to mitigate the immediate impact on Cyrax's psyche and reputation.

It was in this charged atmosphere that Cyrax's notoriety began to expand beyond his usual circles. The Juggalo-adjacent communities, which had been the primary audience for his musical endeavors for nearly a decade, became aware of the controversy surrounding him. This shift in perception set the stage for a significant escalation in Cyrax's online infamy.

The catalyst for this expansion came in the form of an invitation to appear on "The Juggalo Drama Alert," hosted by Fred the Boy Blue. Initially intended as an opportunity for Cyrax to explain his situation with Candle, these appearances quickly morphed into a showcase for Cyrax's unique brand of delusion and drama.

Recognizing the potential for compelling content, Fred had Cyrax appear on multiple episodes in quick succession. This exposure led to an exponential growth in Cyrax's notoriety. Where once he had dealt with one or two occasional impersonators, he now found himself the focus of a dedicated group of trolls.

## The Ascent to Infamy: Cyrax's Troll Infestation

spring and summer of 2019, Chance "Cyrax" Wilkins found himself embroiled in a perfect storm of digital drama, romantic entanglements, and escalating troll activity. The exact timeline of events becomes increasingly murky, a testament to the chaotic nature of Cyrax's online existence.

Around this time, Cyrax began a relationship with a new Heather, not to be confused with his previous paramour of the same name. This new romantic interest would soon become an unwitting player in the unfolding drama of Cyrax's life.

In a moment of uncharacteristic self-awareness, Cyrax produced a video denouncing cyberbullying and other forms of online abuse, warning of the potential for "drastic" consequences. This video, while well-intentioned, would soon take on a darkly ironic tone in light of subsequent events.

The troll community that had begun to coalesce around Cyrax was evolving, moving beyond simple threats and harassment to more sophisticated forms of psychological warfare. One particularly disturbing incident involved a false bomb threat, with trolls calling Cyrax's home phone to claim they had planted an explosive device in Sally's car. This led to a police investigation and, when no device was found, a triumphant video from Cyrax mocking his tormentors.

Realizing that more direct engagement was necessary to extract prime "lolcow" content, some trolls began to infiltrate Cyrax's inner circle. One such individual, known as Boogeyman, managed to establish direct communication with Cyrax, even receiving a voice message detailing the Candle situation.

Concurrently, a Juggalo act called the Bender Boys entered the fray, their involvement earning them the ire of the "Madman of Akron." This escalation was marked by a video edit posted by a channel called Brooklyn Menace, featuring Cyrax wielding a samurai sword, titled "Cyrax Shaolin."

After a month of relentless harassment, the troll community adopted a more insidious approach. Taking a page from the Daniel Larson playbook, they posed as a record label interested in signing Cyrax. This ruse played perfectly into Cyrax's deepest desires and delusions of grandeur.

In late October, Cyrax posted a triumphant video declaring his long-awaited breakthrough:

"See, a lot of people don't realize it, but thanks to the haters over on YouTube on my new channel, I got some exposure. Got hooked up with a major, major underground artist who just happens to be working with some big names in the industry."

This moment of perceived victory was made all the sweeter by the presence of the new Heather at the Cyrax household. Footage from this period shows her kissing Cyrax and joining him in his battles against the trolls. However, the kiss was notable not for its romance, but for Heather's physical reaction - a choke and cough that led trolls to dub Cyrax "trench mouth."

Yet, as had become the pattern in Cyrax's life, this period of triumph was short-lived.

# The Great Label Trolling Saga

October 2019 marked a pivotal moment in the saga of Chance "Cyrax" Wilkins with the emergence of his arch-nemesis and primary tormentor, the self-proclaimed "King of Akron," Music Biz Marty. This new player in Cyrax's digital drama would prove to be a mastermind of manipulation, orchestrating a complex web of deception that would push Cyrax to new heights of desperation and delusion.

Marty's opening gambit was as brilliant as it was cruel. He approached Cyrax under the guise of a benevolent manager interested in handling Cyrax's merchandise. However, this facade quickly gave way to reveal Marty's true persona: a caricature of a greedy, ruthless record executive. In a twist worthy of a soap opera, Marty claimed control over Cyrax's merch store, having allegedly tricked him into signing away the rights to all his merchandise to the fictional "Ram Ranch Records."

The psychological toll of this betrayal was evident in a video from this period, where Cyrax can be seen pleading with Marty to cease his machinations. "You are degrading me, you're ruining my image as an artist, as a person," Cyrax wailed, his voice cracking with emotion. "You are sick!"

To further confound Cyrax, Marty created a false dichotomy between Ram Ranch Records and Bender Boy Records, both of which he secretly controlled. This elaborate ruse played perfectly into Cyrax's paranoia and desperation for success in the music industry.

The period was rife with Cyrax's appearances on various Juggalo-themed shows, including a surreal freestyle session where he attempted to diss Marty while a Juggalette named GCI twerked to his questionable bars. The absurdity of the situation was lost on no one except, perhaps, Cyrax himself.

Early November saw the culmination of Marty and the Bender Boys' elaborate setup. Cyrax, believing he had successfully escaped the clutches of Ram Ranch Records, jubilantly announced his signing with Bender Boy Records. This "victory" came mere weeks after his supposed signing with another label, a fact that seemed to escape Cyrax's notice entirely.

To celebrate this illusory triumph, Cyrax posted what would become one of the most iconic videos in his online saga. Dressed in an oversized pleather jacket and sunglasses, incongruously set against the stark white walls of his bedroom (dubbed by trolls as his "insane asylum containment zone"), Cyrax affected the air of a successful rap mogul. He sipped a non-alcoholic beige liquid as if it were fine champagne and proceeded to give shout-outs to seemingly everyone he'd ever encountered, as though accepting a Grammy.

Perhaps most notably, Cyrax adopted a bizarre, affected New York accent and mannerisms, punctuating his speech with dramatic removals of his sunglasses. He spoke of how his deal with BBR would help him care for "his kids" - children that he neither had nor was likely capable of fathering, presumably referring to his new girlfriend Heather's offspring.

The charade reached its zenith with the release of Cyrax's new single and music video, a contractual obligation to BBR. The song, predictably, was a cacophonous disaster that failed to resonate with any audience beyond Cyrax's dedicated band of trolls.

It was at this moment that the other shoe dropped. In a carefully orchestrated call, representatives from Bender Boy Records informed Cyrax that due to his single's abysmal performance, they had deemed him "unmanageable" and sold his contract. Cyrax's reaction was a mixture of disbelief and rage: "Are you serious right now, bro? You're stupid! I put in all that hard work for you and the crew for what?"

The punchline of this elaborate joke was revealed: Cyrax and his music were now the intellectual property of none other than Music Biz Marty himself. This twist of fate, orchestrated by the very trolls who had been tormenting him, set the stage for an even more tumultuous period in Cyrax's life.

His desperate quest for fame and recognition had led him into a labyrinth of fake record deals and manufactured drama, with Music Biz Marty emerging as the puppet master pulling the strings. The stage was set for an escalation of the Cyrax saga, promising even more outlandish behavior and increasingly dire consequences for the self-proclaimed artist from Akron.

## The Descent into Chaos

2019 drew to a close, and the saga of Chance "Cyrax" Wilkins took a dark and disturbing turn, with his relationship with Heather becoming the focal point of escalating drama and alleged violence. The lines between Cyrax's online persona and real-life actions became increasingly blurred, leading to a series of troubling incidents that would set the stage for an even more tumultuous year ahead.

Heather's presence in Cyrax's life and livestreams added a new dimension to his online infamy. While her romantic interest in Cyrax seemed questionable at best, her apparent desire for attention, even if negative, perfectly aligned with Cyrax's own desperate need for validation in the digital realm.

On November 22nd, the volatile nature of their relationship became public when an anonymous troll reported to the police that Cyrax was being "mean and violent" to Heather, allegedly taking her phone by force. This call, while initially dismissed as a prank, would prove to be eerily prophetic.

Just three days later, on November 25th, another police report was filed, this time by someone named Mike, claiming that Cyrax had hit his girlfriend during a YouTube livestream. While no video evidence has been found to corroborate this specific incident, it marked a significant escalation in the allegations against Cyrax.

The following day, during another livestream, viewers witnessed a disturbing scene as Cyrax aggressively attempted to yank a phone from Heather's hands. This incident prompted yet another call to the Akron Police Department, resulting in a welfare check. The police report from this incident noted that Heather had acknowledged Cyrax's abuse to the person she was streaming with, adding credence to the growing concerns about their relationship.

As if the situation wasn't complex enough, an investigation into Heather's background revealed a tangled web of relationships. Jessica, Heather's former wife, disclosed in an interview that Heather had left her and their two children to pursue a relationship with "DJ Shadowblade" - Cyrax's alter ego.

2020 was approaching, and it became painfully clear that any semblance of normalcy in Cyrax's life was rapidly evaporating. His existence had become a grotesque spectacle, fueled by the relentless activity of malicious trolls and his own self-destructive behavior. Cyrax's once diverse interests and hobbies had been entirely supplanted by an obsessive focus on livestreaming and engaging with his digital tormentors, whether they posed as fans or openly mocked him.

The nadir of this period came in late December 2019, when Cyrax was seen "boxing" via Google Hangouts with someone named Suplex City VOG - a surreal and pathetic display that perfectly encapsulated the depths to which his life had sunk.

The toxic combination of his volatile relationship with Heather, the constant barrage of troll activity, and his own deteriorating mental state promised a 2020 that would push the boundaries of online infamy to new and troubling extremes.

The story of Chance "Cyrax" Wilkins had transformed from a tale of misguided musical ambition into a dark chronicle of abuse, delusion, and digital torment. As the calendar turned to 2020, those who had been following Cyrax's downward spiral braced themselves for what promised to be a year of unprecedented chaos and controversy.

# A New Year of Digital Debauchery

As the calendar turned to January 2020, Chance "Cyrax" Wilkins' descent into internet infamy showed no signs of slowing. The new year began with Cyrax's declaration that he was "becoming a gamer once and for all," a statement that rang hollow given his already extensive use of racial slurs – a hallmark of the toxic gaming culture he seemed eager to embrace.

On January 4th, Cyrax's inability to control his temper was put to the test when he lost a bet with fellow troll Schmeckle Cat. The wager, which allegedly cost Cyrax $100 (a sum many doubted he'd ever possessed), challenged him to maintain his composure against trolls for a week. His failure was as predictable as it was swift.

A video surfaced of Cyrax deriding Jamie Nicole for her inquiries into his alleged abusive behavior and Heather's past. In this tirade, Cyrax referred to Juggalo Records as "Juggis," suggesting a falling out with the community that had long been a part of his online identity. This rift was unsurprising given the label's association with the Bender Boys, who had been instrumental in Cyrax's recent humiliations.

The saga took a more sordid turn on January 12th when explicit photos of Cyrax leaked via Discord. Initially dismissed as fake by some, including the respected Cyrax chronicler CGC, the authenticity of the images was all but confirmed by a commenter presumed to be Heather. Her non-denial denial – claiming Cyrax had been "hacked" while asleep – only added fuel to the fire of speculation. The prevailing theory suggested that Cyrax had been catfished into cheating on Heather, a particularly bold move given that they were cohabiting at the time.

In the aftermath of the leak, Cyrax announced a retreat from online activities. However, this digital detox proved short-lived. Within days, he qualified his statement, committing only to a reduction in livestreams while maintaining his other online presences. He justified this decision by claiming to come from a "family of artists" with "art deep in his blood" – a statement that rang hollow given his family's more notorious history.

Later in the month, Heather and Cyrax returned to streaming, with Heather taking center stage while Cyrax lurked in the background, following her commands. Their content shifted to attacking Jamie Nicole for her coverage of their relationship troubles. In a moment of unintentional comedy, Cyrax's use of a slur prompted Heather to chastise him and send him away so she could "deal with it on her own."

The stream devolved further as Heather accused Jamie of not being a "real Juggalo" – apparently the most scathing insult they could muster. Cyrax, unable to read the room, interjected with homophobic insults directed at Jamie for being a lesbian. This outburst visibly irritated Heather, given her own past relationship with a woman.

This series of events in January 2020 perfectly encapsulated the chaotic and toxic nature of Cyrax's online presence. His inability to maintain composure, his penchant for self-sabotage, and the increasingly dysfunctional nature of his relationship with Heather all pointed to a man spiraling out of control in the digital realm. While his followers and detractors alike watched in morbid fascination, it became clear that Chance "Cyrax" Wilkins was embarking on a year that would push the boundaries of online infamy to new and troubling extremes.

January melted into February 2020, and Chance "Cyrax" Wilkins' online saga continued its descent into absurdity and desperation. The month kicked off with Cyrax and Heather facing criticism from Jamie Nicole over their ill-conceived GoFundMe campaign. The couple's purported goal was to raise money to regain custody of Heather's children from her ex-wife, Jessica. However, the legitimacy of this endeavor was questionable at best, given the legal complexities of custody battles and the couple's less-than-stable living situation.

When Heather wasn't dominating their shared camera time, Cyrax took it upon himself to escalate the conflict with Jamie. In a display of lunacy, he released a "diss video" threatening physical violence against her – a move that only served to further tarnish his already battered reputation.

The irony was palpable when Cyrax, fresh from lamenting how leaked photos of his private parts had ruined his chances of employment or record deals (opportunities that had never genuinely existed for him), was challenged to a fistfight by one of his trolls, Juggalo John. True to form, Cyrax's response was to hide in the attic until his challenger departed, only to emerge later for a staged display of bravado in front of some playground equipment.

In a misguided attempt to reclaim control over his digital persona, Cyrax set his sights on his nemesis, Music Biz Marty, claiming copyright infringement on merchandise – a laughable assertion given that most of the artwork in question was stolen to begin with.

The soap opera of Cyrax's personal life took another turn when, just a day after publicly praising Heather as "the greatest mother in the world," she was seen calling the police to report online threats against

Cyrax. This dysfunctional dynamic painted a picture of a relationship built on mutual exploitation rather than genuine affection.

Cyrax's desperation to control his narrative reached new heights when he created a fake YouTube account under the name "Shadow King." Using a voice changer, he posed as an impartial third party defending himself and Heather against the trolls – a transparent ploy that fooled no one.

February brought news of legal troubles, with Cyrax revealing that Jessica had charged him with civil assault. True to form, he used this development, along with his ongoing troll problems, as excuses for his chronic unemployment.

In a bizarre attempt to settle scores, Cyrax challenged Marty and other trolls to a rap battle. When this predictably failed to yield the desired results, he announced yet another social media hiatus to focus on his "artwork" – a decision he claimed was inspired by a book his great-grandmother had written.

Remarkably, Cyrax managed to stay off social media for exactly one month. However, this absence was more likely due to Sally grounding him and restricting his internet access than any genuine attempt at self-improvement.

On March 15th, Cyrax returned to his online haunts, ready to embark on the next chapter of his digital odyssey.

# Cyrax's Return and Relationship Implosion

His return on March 15th was marked not by a gentle reentry into the online sphere, but by a bombastic accusation against Jessica, Heather's former partner. Cyrax, in his characteristic lack of foresight, branded Jessica a "kidnapper" for denying him and Heather access to her children. This reckless statement set the tone for what would be a tumultuous season in the Cyrax saga.

The ensuing weeks saw a curious absence of Cyrax's usual digital footprint. Speculation among his followers suggested that Sally, his long-suffering adoptive mother, had finally put her foot down. The specter of legal consequences looming over Cyrax's unfiltered online presence seemed to have penetrated even Sally's patient demeanor.

When May rolled around, Cyrax resurfaced with a new persona. Dubbing himself "Scarface" (with an edgy "X" thrown in for good measure), he broadcast from the depths of what appeared to be Sally's basement. His message was a familiar refrain: a farewell to YouTube, citing the ever-present bogeyman of cyberbullying. Yet, in the same breath, he announced plans for a new record label, boasting of predatory profit-sharing schemes that existed only in his mind.

This grand vision was short-lived. Within days, Cyrax sheepishly admitted that his family had staged an intervention of sorts, urging him to step away from his online antics. For a brief moment, it seemed as though Cyrax might heed their advice.

But the siren call of the internet proved too strong. In a whiplash-inducing turn of events, Cyrax declared himself an "e-racer" mere days later, buoyed by a compliment from a retired motorcycle racer about his skills in the videogame Forza Horizon, the least realistic of the Forza racing games series. The irony of this digital "career move" seemed lost on Cyrax.

The real drama, however, was yet to unfold. In a series of increasingly erratic videos, Cyrax chronicled the collapse of his relationship with Heather. His attempts to paint himself as the victim backfired spectacularly, inadvertently revealing his manipulative tactics and emotional instability.

One day, Cyrax would be found "crying" in the dark (a performance as unconvincing as his musical endeavors), lamenting Heather's "cruelty." The next, he would be back to his aggressive posturing, addressing Heather directly in confrontational videos that thinly veiled threats beneath a veneer of "calling out bullshit."

The crescendo of this springtime opera of dysfunction came with Cyrax's shocking admission of physical violence against Heather. This confession, dropped casually in one of his many rambling videos, marked a dark turn in the Cyrax narrative. It was no longer just about internet drama and failed music careers; real-world consequences loomed large.

As May drew to a close, Cyrax's online presence had devolved into a disturbing cycle of aggression, faux remorse, and unintended revelations. His followers watched with a mix of morbid fascination and genuine concern as Cyrax spiraled further into a pit of his own making.

The spring of 2020 had seen Cyrax transition from a figure of online ridicule to something far more troubling. His inability to maintain even the flimsiest facade of stability, coupled with admissions of violence, painted a picture of a man teetering on the edge of a precipice. As summer approached, those invested in the Cyrax saga braced themselves for what promised to be an even more tumultuous chapter in this digital tragedy.

# Cyrax's Violent Tendencies Exposed

The saga of Chance "Cyrax" Wilkins took a sinister turn, revealing a pattern of violence that had long simmered beneath the surface of his online persona. The digital circus that had once been a source of morbid entertainment for his followers now morphed into a disturbing chronicle of real-world aggression and manipulation.

In a series of shocking admissions, Cyrax revealed himself to be what his followers termed an "MO" - a man who resorts to physical violence, particularly choking, when confronted or upset. His modus operandi, as gleaned from his own words, involved not just the act of violence itself but a calculated attempt to evade responsibility. "I blacked out and hurt you one time," he claimed in one video, echoing the excuse he had allegedly used after assaulting his grandmother in 2012. This pattern of violence followed by feigned memory loss painted a chilling picture of Cyrax's mindset.

The facade of contrition was short-lived. Within days, Cyrax was back online, boasting about regaining his "edge." In a chilling video, he declared, "That volatile, dark, evil music that I used to record is coming back, and guess who my first victim's going to be? Ram Ranch Records." The thinly veiled threat, couched in terms of musical rivalry, hinted at a dangerous conflation of his online beefs with real-world aggression.

The culmination of this escalating behavior came in the form of a police report detailing an assault. Cyrax had allegedly punched Heather's brother, Michael, three times as he assisted Heather in moving out. This incident marked a clear escalation from online threats to physical violence against those in his immediate circle.

Following this assault, Cyrax went silent for over a month, likely grappling with the legal and personal fallout of his actions. When he resurfaced in late June, his livestreams took on a new dimension of tension. In one particularly telling moment, Sally, his adoptive mother, briefly appeared on camera. Cyrax's attempt to complain about her presence was met with a dismissive "Wow, that's just too flipping bad" from Sally, hinting at the strained dynamics within the household.

As July began, Cyrax returned to his online activities as if nothing had happened, a pattern all too familiar to his long-time followers. This ability to compartmentalize and ignore the consequences of his actions spoke volumes about his disconnect from reality.

The events of late spring and early summer 2020 marked a turning point in the Cyrax saga. What had once been viewed as the antics of a delusional but ultimately harmless internet personality now took on a darker hue. The line between Cyrax's online persona and his real-world behavior had not just blurred - it had vanished entirely.

As his followers grappled with this new reality, questions arose about the ethical implications of continuing to engage with or document Cyrax's behavior. The entertainment value of his online presence was now overshadowed by genuine concerns for the safety of those in his orbit.

The Cyrax of summer 2020 was no longer just a figure of internet infamy; he had become a cautionary tale about the dangers of unchecked online behavior spilling into real-world violence. As the hot days of July stretched ahead, those invested in the Cyrax story braced themselves for what promised to be an increasingly volatile and potentially dangerous chapter in this digital tragedy.

# The Summer of Delusion

July 2020 dawned, and Chance "Cyrax" Wilkins re-emerged from his latest self-imposed exile with a video titled "New Look, New Attitude, New Me." The irony of claiming a fresh start halfway through the year seemed lost on Cyrax, who sported his grandmother's glasses in a misguided attempt to appear sophisticated. This peculiar fashion choice served as an apt metaphor for Cyrax's distorted view of the world and his place in it.

In a desperate bid to prove his musical legitimacy, Cyrax shared what he claimed was an original beat. The result was a cacophonous mess that assaulted the ears, yet Cyrax proudly declared, "You hear that? That sounds like hard work to me." This delusional self-assessment was followed by grandiose claims of a potential multi-million dollar contract with "very serious record labels" - a fantasy that existed solely in Cyrax's mind.

The depths of Cyrax's ethical bankruptcy were laid bare on July 24th when he confirmed what many had suspected: the $3,000 GoFundMe campaign for Heather's custody battle had been embezzled. While Cyrax conveniently neglected to mention his own misuse of funds, he was quick to throw Heather under the bus, revealing she had spent $500 on wigs.

As summer progressed, Cyrax's behavior became increasingly erratic. He posted a series of videos wielding a stick, ostensibly to prove his fighting prowess and intimidate his nemesis, Music Biz Marty. These displays of faux machismo, punctuated by threats like "I'm the last motherfucker that you want to box with," only served to highlight the growing disconnect between Cyrax's self-image and reality.

August saw Cyrax oscillating between tearful lamentations about accusations of music theft and boasts about his emotional control. In a bewildering twist, he appeared in videos with yet another girlfriend, showcasing a decent microphone setup that belied his claims of financial hardship.

September brought a new low as Cyrax blamed online trolls for his decision to forgo birthday gifts so his family could pay for Sally's medical bills. This attempt to paint himself as a selfless martyr ignored the glaring fact that, at 30 years old, he remained unemployed and dependent on his adoptive mother.

The culmination of this summer of delusion came on September 18th, when Cyrax made two contradictory videos in the same day. The first called for a truce with his trolls, while the second declared war on them for allegedly insulting his "military family" - a family he had previously denounced.

This rapid-fire contradiction exemplified Cyrax's desperate need for attention and conflict. Without the constant engagement from trolls, Cyrax faced a void - a return to the obscurity that had defined his early attempts at online fame.

## A Demonic Ending to 2020

Chance "Cyrax" Wilkins' online presence took a turn towards the increasingly bizarre and unhinged. The man who once dreamed of musical stardom had devolved into a digital caricature, his actions a grotesque pantomime of celebrity and infamy.

October brought with it a peculiar political interlude. Cyrax, never one for coherent commentary, launched into a rambling tirade against Joe Biden in a video cryptically titled "We're All." This foray into punditry was short-lived, as the relentless barrage from his digital tormentors quickly drove him back to familiar ground - the well-worn path of victimhood.

In a tearful video, Cyrax blamed his online antagonists for Sally's high blood pressure, a claim that rang hollow given his steadfast refusal to heed her pleas to log off. This paradoxical behavior - simultaneously bemoaning the consequences of his online presence while clinging desperately to it - became emblematic of Cyrax's digital existence.

As Halloween approached, Cyrax unveiled a shocking claim: his stepfather, Ed, had allegedly overdosed. The timing of this announcement, coinciding conveniently with a scheduled rap battle, raised eyebrows among his followers. Many speculated that this was yet another fabrication, a desperate ploy for sympathy or an elaborate excuse to avoid confrontation.

November heralded a descent into the truly absurd. In a misguided attempt at intimidation, Cyrax placed a call to his nemesis, Music Biz Marty, affecting a demonic possession. His growled threats, far from menacing, came across as a poor imitation of inebriation, further eroding any shred of credibility he might have retained.

The month also saw Cyrax fall victim to yet another catfishing scheme. His eagerness to send explicit videos to "Jasmine," a fictional online persona, led to the collapse of his brief relationship with Caitlyn. The revelation that Cyrax had immediately created a new online account after promising to stay offline spoke volumes about his addiction to digital attention.

In the wake of this latest romantic failure, Cyrax's behavior spiraled further out of control. Allegations surfaced of a botched attempt to hire a hitman to target Music Biz Marty, a claim so outlandish it bordered on the comical, were it not for its serious implications.

As autumn drew to a close, Cyrax's desperation reached new heights. He issued hollow legal threats against Marty, claiming copyright infringement in a last-ditch effort to silence his critics. In a final, melodramatic flourish, Cyrax declared himself a "soulless demon," whispering menacingly from the shadows in a video that seemed to mark his complete detachment from reality.

This autumnal period in the Cyrax saga served as a stark illustration of the potential dangers of unchecked internet notoriety. As winter loomed on the horizon, those who had followed Cyrax's digital odyssey were left to wonder what new depths of delusion and despair awaited in the coming months. The man who had once aspired to be a musical sensation had become a cautionary tale, a digital specter haunting the fringes of internet infamy.

As 2020 drew to a close, Chance "Cyrax" Wilkins' digital saga took on an increasingly dark and disturbing tone. The winter months saw him spiraling further into a realm of paranoia and delusion, with his obsession over his ex-girlfriend Heather reaching new, unsettling heights.

Half a year after Heather's departure, Cyrax unleashed a video that plumbed new depths of desperation. In a performance as unconvincing as it was troubling, he feigned tears while claiming Heather was pregnant with his child. According to his narrative, she planned to put the baby up for state custody, denying Cyrax any access. This fabricated drama, likely concocted by trolls and eagerly embraced by Cyrax, showcased his increasing disconnect from reality.

In a follow-up video that stretched for an excruciating hour and fifteen minutes, Cyrax's approach to this supposedly serious situation was to hurl invectives at Heather while playing Forza Horizon. The incongruity between the gravity of his claims and the casual nature of his gaming session spoke volumes about his mental state.

Cyrax claimed to have called Heather about their supposed child, only to be met with denial. Rather than considering the obvious - that he had been duped by his online tormentors - he labeled Heather a "pathological liar." This willingness to believe the most outlandish scenarios over simple truths had become a hallmark of Cyrax's worldview.

The implausibility of Cyrax and Heather conceiving a child was lost on no one who remembered Heather's visceral reaction to Cyrax's notorious "trench mouth." Yet, Cyrax clung to this fantasy with a fervor that bordered on the pathological.

In a particularly unsettling development, Cyrax revealed that he had sent Sally and Ed to confront Heather at her workplace, resulting in their being banned from the premises. This use of his parents as proxies in his personal vendettas highlighted both his cowardice and his willingness to drag others into his delusional crusades.

The creep factor escalated when Cyrax recorded a freestyle rap dedicated to his non-existent unborn child. This bizarre tribute to an imaginary offspring underscored the depths of his detachment from reality.

When Music Biz Marty claimed to know Heather's whereabouts, Cyrax's response was immediate and violent. He threatened to "beat Marty's ass," boasting that he could do so at will. This tough-guy posturing, a stark contrast to his earlier tearful performances, exemplified the mercurial nature of Cyrax's online persona.

## A New Year Of Spiraling

As the clock struck midnight on December 31st, 2020, Chance "Cyrax" Wilkins' digital saga took yet another bizarre turn. The arrival of a bundle of rope in his mail sparked an inexplicable outburst, setting the tone for what would be a year of escalating absurdity and concern.

The dawn of 2021 found Cyrax adopting an inexplicable Irish accent, a bewildering choice that left his followers scratching their heads. "It's your boy B to do a little bit of practice on some F1 2020," he declared, his faux brogue as unconvincing as his claims of musical prowess.

While January passed with relative quiet, February brought a slew of troubling developments. Reports emerged of rats infesting Cyrax's humble abode, a fitting metaphor for the deteriorating state of his life. More alarmingly, his basement bed fell victim to a bed bug infestation, a situation that Cyrax claimed was severely impacting his health.

In his never-ending feud with Music Biz Marty, Cyrax made the ill-advised decision to invoke the symbolism of a notorious political party, a move that showcased his willingness to court controversy at any cost. "Going to do some Ramstein," he declared ominously, oblivious to the implications of his words.

Cyrax's romantic life took another strange turn when he entered into a relationship with "Tangerine Cat," unaware that his new paramour was actually a long-term covert troll working for Marty. This development came on the heels of Cyrax being catfished into confessing a disturbing fantasy involving Snickers bars and bodily functions, a revelation that left even his most hardened followers aghast.

Mid-February saw Cyrax escalate his threats against Marty and another troll,

Schmeckle Cat, claiming he would use his stepfather Ed's rifle to "carry out a hit." This dangerous rhetoric marked a new low in Cyrax's online behavior, blurring the lines between digital drama and real-world threats.

As Cyrax approached the 1,000 subscriber mark on YouTube, his followers orchestrated a cruel prank. They mass subscribed with troll accounts, allowing Cyrax to briefly celebrate his "achievement," only to unsubscribe en masse moments later. Cyrax's reaction was predictably volatile, peppered with racial slurs and accusations.

In a move that perfectly encapsulated his disconnect from reality, Cyrax convinced Sally to call the police about his online "cyberbullying." The resulting police report painted a picture of exasperated law enforcement, familiar with Cyrax's antics and increasingly tired of his baseless complaints. "Nothing I was told today was a crime," the report concluded, a damning indictment of Cyrax's attempts to weaponize law enforcement against his online tormentors.

## March Madness

March 2021 unfolded and Chance "Cyrax" Wilkins' digital existence spiraled into a maelstrom of violence, threats, and medical mishaps that would make even the most hardened internet observers wince.

On March 5th, during a live stream with his nemesis Marty, his girlfriend Tangerine Cat, and fellow troll Lava, Cyrax reached his breaking point. In a display of childish rage, he destroyed a gift from Lava, screaming threats that chilled even his most desensitized followers:

"I swear to God, if you don't stop, I swear to God I will hunt you down and beat your ass within an inch of your life," Cyrax bellowed, his face contorted with fury. "Lava, you better hope I don't know where you live, otherwise you're gonna be six feet under. And same with you, Marty. I know where you live, so don't test me!"

His tirade culminated in him smashing an ocarina against his wall, leaving holes that would serve as a visible reminder of his outburst in future videos. This act of destruction marked a new low in Cyrax's increasingly volatile behavior.

But the real bombshell came when Marty broke the news of Cyrax's hospitalization for a fungal infection on his genitals. The cause, as grotesque as it was tragic, was reportedly Cyrax's habit of neglecting personal hygiene after frequent self-gratification, leading to chafing and infection. This deeply personal medical issue became fodder for online ridicule, with Cyrax later appearing on Marty's stream to berate everyone for discussing his condition.

In a moment of unintentional comedy that bordered on the absurd, it was revealed that Cyrax required his adoptive mother, Sally, to apply the medicinal cream to his affected areas. This dependency on Sally for such an intimate task spoke volumes about Cyrax's stunted development and lack of self-sufficiency.

The month was punctuated by a series of police reports that painted a picture of a household in crisis. Welfare checks, reports of online threats, and domestic disturbances became routine. One particularly troubling incident involved Cyrax and his stepfather Ed getting into a physical altercation, resulting in Sally calling the police.

The aftermath of this fight was captured during another of Marty's streams, where Cyrax appeared with a bloodied mouth, screaming about how he had almost taken his own life due to the bullying he was experiencing. This shocking appearance provided a glimpse into the real-world consequences of Cyrax's online behavior and the toll it was taking on his family relationships.

March drew to a close while Cyrax's world continued to crumble. Ed left the household, unable to cope with Cyrax's antics, which Cyrax predictably blamed on the trolls. Even his relationship with Tangerine Cat, his digital girlfriend, was on the verge of collapse.

## The Great Stylus Incident

The departure of Tangerine Cat, driven away by Cyrax's indiscriminate sharing of explicit images to multiple trolls claiming to be women, barely registered before a new digital paramour emerged. Enter "Strawberry Sunshine," a persona that would push Cyrax to new lows of degradation and self-harm.

Within a month of their "relationship," Strawberry had convinced Cyrax to engage in an act so grotesque and self-debasing that it defies polite description. Suffice to say, it involved a stylus and a part of Cyrax's anatomy never meant to accommodate such an object. This incident, while too graphic to detail, became part of the Cyrax lore, a testament to his willingness to debase himself for online attention.

Concurrent with the Strawberry saga, Cyrax fell victim to another catfishing scheme. This time, he sent explicit images to someone posing as "Cindy Lou," a fictional transgender individual with cognitive challenges. This behavior showcased Cyrax's utter lack of discernment and his willingness to exploit perceived vulnerability for his own gratification.

In response to the growing chorus of criticism, Cyrax resorted to his familiar tactic of threatening self-harm. However, his attempts at manipulation reached new levels of absurdity when he brandished not a knife, but the very stylus involved in his earlier degradation. This pitiful display, far from eliciting sympathy, only served to underscore the depths of his desperation.

Undeterred by the failure of his stylus-wielding theatrics, Cyrax repeated the performance multiple times over the following days. The culmination of this pathetic display was Strawberry Sunshine ending their "relationship" on April 20th, leaving Cyrax once again alone in his digital wasteland.

Whispers of an even darker chapter in the Cyrax saga began to circulate. Rumors of inappropriate interactions with a purported minor sent shockwaves through his online community, promising a reckoning that could have real-world legal consequences.

This period in Cyrax's digital odyssey served as a stark reminder of the potential dangers lurking in the darker corners of the internet. His willingness to engage in increasingly degrading acts for attention, coupled with his apparent inability to discern reality from fantasy, painted a troubling picture of a man spiraling out of control.

As his followers braced themselves for what promised to be the most disturbing chapter yet in the Cyrax saga, questions of ethics and complicity began to surface. How long could this digital trainwreck continue before real-world authorities intervened? And at what point does observing and documenting such behavior cross the line into enabling?

The stage is now set for the darkest moment in Cyrax's internet saga.

# Cyrax's Darkest Hour

As spring 2021 progressed, the saga of Chance "Cyrax" Wilkins plunged into depths so dark and disturbing that even his most hardened followers were left aghast. The line between digital provocateur and potential predator blurred in ways that demanded serious scrutiny.

The month began with Cyrax's increasingly tiresome stylus antics reaching new lows of depravity. Frustrated by his predictable shock tactics, his tormentors decided to raise the stakes. Masshole Report, a troll outlet, set up an elaborate sting operation, posing as "Crystal," a purported 14-year-old girl struggling with bullying.

Cyrax's response to this bait was swift and alarming. He showered the decoy with compliments, declared his love, and bizarrely claimed that despite being 30, he looked 14 himself. What followed was a series of exchanges so inappropriate and potentially criminal that they cannot be detailed here. Suffice to say, Cyrax's behavior towards someone he believed to be a minor crossed every conceivable line of decency and legality.

This was no isolated incident. Further investigation revealed a pattern of similar behavior dating back to 2014 when Cyrax, then 24, had engaged in equally troubling online interactions. Another revelation involved a brief relationship with a 15-year-old named Khloe, adding to the growing list of concerns about Cyrax's proclivities.

As the walls closed in, Cyrax's tactics became increasingly desperate. In a misguided attempt to silence his critics, he resorted to exposing himself on camera during one of Marty's streams, hoping to get the channel shut down for nudity. This tactic, as ill-conceived as it was illegal, became a recurring theme in his arsenal of self-destructive behaviors.

The situation reached a fever pitch when Sally, apparently aware of the brewing storm, called the police over a fake picture of someone holding a firearm outside their house. This attempt to deflect attention from Cyrax's online activities spoke volumes about the household's growing desperation.

In a twist that could only be described as darkly ironic, Cyrax's father, recently released from prison, discovered his son's infamy as an internet lolcow. His appearance on one of Marty's streams might have been comical if not for the disturbing revelations that followed. A Pinterest account linked to Cyrax's father, under the name Oenus Ravenwood, contained categories with deeply troubling themes related to the sexualization of minors. When confronted, he claimed it was for "Trans kid awareness," a defense as flimsy as it was offensive.

This chapter in the Cyrax saga marked a turning point. What had once been viewed as the antics of a delusional but ultimately harmless internet personality now took on a sinister hue. The entertainment value of following Cyrax's online presence was overshadowed by genuine concerns about public safety and the welfare of vulnerable individuals.

Those who had followed the Cyrax story found themselves grappling with difficult questions. At what point does observing and documenting such behavior become complicity? How long could this digital trainwreck continue before real-world authorities intervened in a meaningful way?

The Cyrax saga had transformed from a cautionary tale about internet fame into something far darker – a stark reminder of the potential dangers lurking in the digital shadows. As his followers watched in horror, it became clear that the story of Chance "Cyrax" Wilkins was approaching a reckoning that could have far-reaching consequences both online and in the real world.

# Redemption and Relapse

While the summer of 2021 unfolded, Chance "Cyrax" Wilkins embarked on a journey of supposed spiritual awakening, peppered with his usual bouts of delusion and self-victimization. In a move that surprised even his most jaded followers, Cyrax turned to Christianity, apparently seeking redemption for his myriad transgressions.

This newfound faith, however, proved as superficial as his musical aspirations. Cyrax's interpretation of Christian values manifested in a series of spoken word poems that cast him as a misunderstood victim – a far cry from the teachings of humility and repentance central to the faith he claimed to embrace.

In a display of misguided loyalty, Cyrax rekindled his friendship with Chuck Steagle, defending him against various accusations. This alliance with a similarly controversial figure raised eyebrows among those who hoped Cyrax's religious turn might lead to genuine change.

Physical signs of Cyrax's deteriorating living conditions became increasingly apparent. Frequent head-scratching during his videos revealed an ongoing battle with bed bugs, a grim reminder of the squalor that had become his daily reality.

In a moment of unexpected diplomacy, Cyrax struck a deal with his nemesis, Music Biz Marty. In exchange for the return of his PayPal account, Cyrax agreed to a face-to-face meeting to settle their differences. True to form, when Marty arrived at Cyrax's home, our protagonist retreated to his attic hideout, his bravado evaporating in the face of real-world confrontation.

During this period, a moment of unintentional comedy arose when Cyrax revealed the paltry fruits of his musical labor – a lifetime earnings of just under $6. This pitiful sum stood as a stark testament to the gulf between Cyrax's grandiose self-image and his actual impact on the music world.

The specter of Cyrax's past indiscretions loomed large when a Chris Hansen impersonator confronted him online. The exchange, reminiscent of Hansen's "To Catch a Predator" series, served as a chilling reminder of the allegations that continued to dog Cyrax.

In yet another relationship twist, Cyrax announced his engagement to Trisha, a transgender woman. His vehement defense of her against online trolls who misgendered her seemed at odds with his previous behavior, leaving many to wonder about the sincerity of this latest romantic entanglement.

Cyrax's ongoing feud with Marty took another comical turn when he posted videos of himself "training" for a fight, only to once again cower when Marty actually showed up. In a display of cowardice masquerading as filial piety, Cyrax sent Ed and Sally to confront Marty in his stead.

The chapter reached its absurdist peak when Cyrax attempted to link a local shooting, which injured a 13-year-old, to Marty's "goons." This outlandish claim, devoid of any evidence, showcased Cyrax's propensity for manufacturing drama and his desperate need to cast himself as the central figure in every local tragedy.

It became clear that Cyrax's attempts at redemption were as hollow as his musical career. His spiritual journey, like so many of his endeavors, seemed destined to be another footnote in the ongoing tragicomedy of his online existence. Those who followed the Cyrax saga were left to wonder what new depths of delusion and self-sabotage awaited in the chapters to come.

# Cyrax's Edless Spiral

January 2022 brought a stark reminder of the real-world consequences of Cyrax's online obsession. During one of his streams, viewers were treated to the unsettling sound of Cyrax arguing with Sally, his long-suffering adoptive mother. Her pleas for him to find employment were met with delusional claims about the importance of "protecting his family" online. This exchange laid bare the dysfunction at the heart of the Cyrax household, where internet fame had superseded basic adult responsibilities.

February marked a new low in Cyrax's online behavior. In an incident reminiscent of DarksydePhil's infamous faux pas, Cyrax inadvertently broadcast himself engaging in self-gratification during a live stream.

While the visual content was mercifully obscured, the audio left little to the imagination. Adding a layer of pathos to the situation, it became apparent that Cyrax was viewing old videos of Heather, a ghost from his romantic past, during this private moment turned public spectacle.

The aftermath of this incident cast a pall over Cyrax's online presence, with many of his followers questioning the ethical implications of continuing to engage with his content.

In a bizarre turn of events, Marty, Cyrax's longtime digital nemesis, managed to lure him back online by spreading rumors of Cyrax's demise and replacement by an AI dubbed "AIrax." This elaborate ruse spoke volumes about Cyrax's inability to disengage from the toxic online environment that had come to define his existence.

April brought a new chapter in Cyrax's ongoing drama when his house was visited by law enforcement. True to form, Cyrax greatly exaggerated the nature of this encounter, painting a picture of a high-stakes raid complete with armed officers and imminent danger. "There would be 10 cops outside with guns pointed at me," he claimed dramatically. The reality, as often was the case with Cyrax, was far more mundane – a simple questioning with flashlights rather than firearms.

This embellishment of real-world events highlighted Cyrax's growing disconnect from reality. His need to inject drama and danger into every aspect of his life spoke to a deep-seated desire for relevance and attention, no matter the cost.

The Cyrax saga had evolved from a tale of misguided musical ambition into a troubling chronicle of a life consumed by internet infamy. His inability to maintain healthy boundaries, both online and off, had transformed what was once viewed as harmless entertainment into a concerning spectacle of self-destruction.

Those who had followed Cyrax's story for years found themselves grappling with difficult questions. At what point does observing such behavior cross the line into enabling? How much further could this digital trainwreck progress before real-world interventions became necessary?

As 2022 progressed, Chance "Cyrax" Wilkins' digital saga took increasingly bizarre and disturbing turns, cementing his status as an internet spectacle of the most troubling kind.

May brought a new low in Cyrax's online presence when he audibly defecated during a live stream. His nonchalant reaction - "Sh*t guys, it's storming out" - spoke volumes about the desensitization that years of internet infamy had wrought.

June saw Cyrax oscillating between victimhood and aggression. In a video where he feigned tears and played the victim, he simultaneously issued threats of violence, even against law enforcement. "So help me God, if you cops don't do something about this, I will," he raged, "and trust me when I say the end result isn't going to be pretty." This jarring juxtaposition of vulnerability and aggression highlighted the increasingly unstable nature of Cyrax's online persona.

By October, Cyrax's notoriety had reached unprecedented heights. Danny Brown, a renowned rapper, publicly expressed his fascination with the Cyrax saga. Brown's description of Cyrax as a "little touched up guy" from Ohio who was constantly reinventing himself captured the essence of Cyrax's appeal to a certain subset of internet culture. The rapper's recounting of the elaborate ruse to lure Cyrax back online by faking his death underscored the parasocial relationship that had developed between Cyrax and his audience.

In a surreal twist, Chris Chan's impersonator, "Liquid Chris," entered the fray, accusing Cyrax of copying the infamous Chris Chan. This meta-moment of internet lore colliding highlighted the incestuous nature of online infamy.

The year culminated in perhaps the most invasive violation of Cyrax's privacy yet. His Facebook account was genuinely hacked, leading to the discovery of a video so intimately degrading that it defies description in polite company... Where he licks his own... well...

As 2022 drew to a close and 2023 dawned, Chance "Cyrax" Wilkins' saga continued its relentless descent into chaos and despair. The final chapter of this digital tragedy unfolded with a series of events that pushed the boundaries of credulity and human endurance.

December 2022 brought reports of another physical altercation between Cyrax and his stepfather Ed, a grim reminder of the volatile home environment that had become Cyrax's reality. In the aftermath, Cyrax claimed to have developed stress-related eczema, which escalated into a full-blown leg infection. This physical deterioration mirrored his ongoing mental and emotional decline.

The new year began with Cyrax falling victim to yet another cruel prank. Tricked into inserting a contaminated USB stick into his Xbox, he destroyed his primary source of entertainment and connection to the online world. In a moment of surreal comedy, his nemesis Marty convinced him to perform a "dance" to magically repair the console, a request Cyrax complied with in his desperation.

Cyrax's penchant for baseless accusations reached new heights when he repeatedly labeled rapper Danny Brown a pedophile, prompting threats of legal action. This reckless behavior seemed to stem from a place of utter desperation, a man with nothing left to lose.

In a surprising turn of events, Cyrax's longstanding feud with Marty culminated in an actual physical confrontation. Despite losing the fight, Cyrax immediately took to streaming, attempting to spin his defeat into a moral victory for simply showing up. This cognitive dissonance highlighted his inability to confront reality, even in the face of undeniable physical evidence.

2023 progressed and Cyrax's living conditions deteriorated to shocking levels. His ex-girlfriend Jasmine revealed disturbing details about his hygiene and living space, including his habit of popping and sniffing bed bugs, cohabitating with mice, and eating food crawling with roaches. These revelations painted a picture of a man living in squalor, both physically and mentally.

The Wilkins family's financial troubles came to a head with the threat of eviction, adding another layer of instability to Cyrax's already chaotic existence. In a final act of violence, Cyrax assaulted a visiting troll with a bat, leading to his arrest and subsequent release on bond.

Another chapter of the Cyrax saga draws to a close, and the future remains uncertain but undoubtedly bleak. Without serious intervention and institutionalization, it seems likely that Cyrax will continue down this path of self-destruction. His apparent inability to comprehend the concept of "winning" or to care about the consequences of his actions suggests that this cycle of attention-seeking behavior and conflict will persist indefinitely.

The tragedy of Chance "Cyrax" Wilkins serves as a stark cautionary tale about the dark side of internet fame and the potential consequences of unchecked mental health issues in the digital age. His story challenges us to consider the ethics of online engagement and the role of observers in perpetuating cycles of digital exploitation.

Cyrax continues to growl at his computer monitor, locked in endless conflict with unseen adversaries, while we are left to ponder the nature of internet culture and our own complicity in the creation and perpetuation of figures like Cyrax. His saga, seemingly without end, stands as a testament to the complex and often troubling intersection of technology, mental health, and human nature in the 21st century.

# The LolcowLive Spectacle

As 2024 unfolded, the saga of Chance "Cyrax" Wilkins took an unexpected turn when he found himself in the spotlight of the infamous LolcowLive Podcast. Hosted by internet-genius Keemstar and featuring internet personalities TommyC, Wingsofredemption, and Boogie2988 (Wings and Boogie being lolcow themselves) this June 2nd event promised to be a watershed moment in the Cyrax narrative.

The podcast began with an air of surreal normality. Cyrax, seemingly oblivious to the true nature of the gathering, introduced himself with his trademark bravado. "Hey, like I always tell everybody, call me whatever you want, just don't call me late for dinner, man," he quipped, showcasing the mix of forced humor and desperation that had become his hallmark.

As the conversation unfolded, Cyrax regaled the hosts with his version of his rise to internet infamy. "I started out doing music back in like 2009," he explained, "but never in my whole career of being on YouTube and doing music like I've been doing over the years, never did I think that I would ever get drug into this massively crazy situation that I got drugged into."

The hosts, playing along with the charade, prodded Cyrax about his music and his experiences with online trolling. Cyrax, ever eager for attention, boasted about his ability to handle criticism and dish out diss tracks. "If somebody were to throw a diss track at me, I could easily take whatever they say and spin it," he claimed, oblivious to the irony of his situation.

As the interview progressed, Cyrax's disconnect from reality became increasingly apparent. He spoke of his "haters" with a mix of disdain and perverse pride, failing to recognize that his notoriety stemmed not from admiration but from morbid fascination with his ongoing digital spectacle.

The conversation took a turn when the topic of Music Biz Marty, Cyrax's longtime nemesis, arose. Cyrax's demeanor shifted as he recounted their conflicts, including the infamous confrontation at Marty's Airbnb. "I rolled up on him because I got tired of him sparking his shit mouth," Cyrax boasted, seemingly proud of his ill-advised aggression despite the physical disparity between them.

The hosts skillfully probed deeper into Cyrax's confrontation with Music Biz Marty, revealing the layers of delusion and contradictions that defined Cyrax's worldview.

When questioned about the alleged loss of a tooth during the fight, as reported on Kiwi Farms, Cyrax vehemently denied it. His recounting of the altercation bordered on the absurd, describing Marty, a man nearly twice his size, "slipping" and falling on top of him. "It didn't really hurt having him fall," Cyrax claimed, "what hurt was the impact of my body meeting the ground at such a velocity."

The hosts, particularly Boogie2988, astutely pointed out the inconsistencies in Cyrax's narrative. They suggested that Marty's entire strategy might have been to provoke Cyrax into doing something stupid. Cyrax, in a moment of unexpected clarity, acknowledged this possibility but quickly reverted to his street-tough persona: "When you f*** around with the wrong s***, chances are you're gonna get it."

The conversation took a surreal turn when Cyrax announced he was working to have Marty's YouTube channel shut down. He boasted about gathering evidence and contacting YouTube staff, claiming FBI involvement was imminent. The hosts, drawing from their own experiences with online harassment and YouTube policies, gently tried to temper Cyrax's expectations.

Cyrax's reasoning for not pressing charges against Marty further highlighted his disconnected worldview. He cited the fight occurring on public property and invoked street code: "When you're from the streets, you don't go to the cops." This statement, coming from a self-described "army brat," drew skeptical reactions from the hosts.

Throughout this segment, Cyrax's responses oscillated between tough-guy bravado and naive optimism. His inability to recognize the futility of his actions or the potential consequences of his ongoing feud with Marty painted a picture of a man trapped in a cycle of his own making.

As the interview continued, it became increasingly clear that Cyrax's participation in the LolcowLive podcast was not just entertainment for the hosts and audience, but a stark illustration of the complex issues surrounding internet fame, online harassment, and the exploitation of individuals like Cyrax for content. The hosts' careful navigation of Cyrax's contradictory statements and delusional beliefs set the stage for the eventual confrontation that would force Cyrax to face the harsh realities of his online behavior.

As the LolcowLive podcast delved deeper into Cyrax's world, a tapestry of contradictions and delusions began to unfold. The hosts, particularly Boogie2988, skillfully navigated Cyrax's narratives, exposing the fragile constructs of his perceived reality.

The conversation turned to Cyrax's recent legal troubles, stemming from an incident where he allegedly assaulted someone with a baseball bat. Cyrax's recounting of the event was a study in cognitive dissonance. He initially claimed the incident occurred on his property, a justification for his actions under the "Castle Doctrine."

However, when pressed, he admitted it happened on the sidewalk - a public easement.

Cyrax attempted to justify his actions by painting a picture of a mob descending on his property. "He actually gathered up like half our neighborhood to show up to my house to harass me and my family," Cyrax claimed. Yet, when questioned about the video evidence, he conceded that the alleged attacker was "almost by himself."

The hosts gently but persistently pointed out the legal and logical flaws in Cyrax's reasoning. They emphasized that even if someone is trespassing, physical assault is not a legal response. Cyrax's attempts to reconcile his actions with his self-image as a "street-smart army brat" only served to highlight his disconnection from reality.

The discussion then shifted to a more alarming incident - an alleged shooting near Cyrax's home. His claim that police refused to investigate bullet holes in his window strained credibility. "Next day we ended up calling the cops after I had watched back the footage and I had seen the bullet holes," Cyrax stated, seemingly unaware of the implausibility of police ignoring such a serious incident.

Perhaps the most revealing moment came when Cyrax was asked about the most disturbing thing trolls had done to him. His response was both shocking and dubious: "They ended up sending a dead baby pig still in the mother's fetal sack in a cardboard box, bloody and all." This claim, while horrifying if true, seemed to be another example of Cyrax's tendency towards exaggeration.

The hosts' reactions to this story were telling. Boogie's inappropriate joke about eating the pig hinted at the skepticism underlying their engagement with Cyrax. The follow-up story about a mysterious powder that prompted a Hazmat response further illustrated Cyrax's propensity for dramatic narratives.

As the LolcowLive podcast reached its climax, the tone shifted dramatically. The hosts, who had been gently probing Cyrax's stories, suddenly took a more confrontational approach, addressing the most serious allegations against him.

The conversation turned to Cyrax's love life, with the hosts inquiring about his relationship history. Cyrax began by discussing a woman named Candle, describing a convoluted situation involving online drama and accusations. His narrative was disjointed and self-contradictory, painting himself as a victim of false allegations.

However, the hosts quickly steered the conversation to more troubling territory – Cyrax's history of being catfished, particularly by individuals claiming to be underage. When confronted about interactions with a purported 14-year-old girl, Cyrax's responses became increasingly evasive and contradictory.

Cyrax initially attempted to deflect, claiming that these incidents were fabrications by his nemesis, Marty. He stated, "Marty had hired Masshole Mafia to talk to me the way that she did on the phone call. She pretended to be 18, tricked me into sending certain photos, and it was only after the photos were sent that she claimed to be underage."

However, the hosts pressed further, revealing they had access to text conversations that contradicted Cyrax's version of events. When confronted with evidence that he had knowingly engaged with someone claiming to be 14, Cyrax's excuses became more desperate and implausible.

"A lot of these people, they like to photoshop shit, dude. I'm not joking," Cyrax claimed, attempting to discredit the evidence against him. He even suggested that AI technology had been used to fabricate voice recordings of him saying inappropriate things to young women.

The hosts, particularly Boogie2988, became increasingly frustrated with Cyrax's evasions. "Come on, chance, let's be honest here," Boogie pressed, referencing a video where Cyrax had admitted to recent interactions with underage girls.

As Cyrax continued to deny and deflect, the atmosphere in the podcast became tense. The hosts' tone shifted from curiosity to outright condemnation. "You keep falling for 14... they clearly state that they're 14 years old, and you keep going for it," one host accused.

Cyrax's attempts to justify his actions became increasingly incoherent. He tried to argue that the individuals weren't actually underage, despite acknowledging that they claimed to be. His contradictions and evasions only served to further incriminate him in the eyes of the hosts and audience.

The confrontation reached its peak when one host bluntly stated, "You are so fucked, dude. Like, what's your deal?" Cyrax's response, a desperate attempt to deflect attention to Boogie, marked the complete unraveling of his facade.

Chapter Title: "The Meltdown and Aftermath: Cyrax's Explosive Exit"

As the interview reached its boiling point, Cyrax's composure completely shattered. His face contorted with rage, he unleashed a torrent of profanity-laced insults at the hosts, particularly targeting Tommy. "You're a small piece of shit," Cyrax snarled, his eyes wild with anger. "You're an internet fucking shit talker that thinks he knows everything!"

The hosts, particularly Boogie2988, attempted to de-escalate the situation, but Cyrax was beyond reason. When Boogie tried to interject with questions from Discord members, Cyrax erupted, "You fucking Mong looking motherfucker!" This outburst marked the point of no return.

Cyrax's rant became increasingly incoherent as he oscillated between defending himself and attacking the hosts. "I don't give a fuck what people post around, bro!" he shouted, even as his actions betrayed his words. His desperation became palpable as he tried to deflect attention to other alleged predators, insisting, "There's a difference between getting caught up in what I got caught up in and someone like Tony who's actually done real shit!"

As the hosts pressed him on his interactions with underage girls, Cyrax's defenses crumbled. His attempts to claim he was being framed or targeted by AI technology fell flat in the face of the evidence presented. In a final, desperate move, he invoked law enforcement, claiming, "I've had FBI and detectives, they've all three said the same thing that I am not a [predator]!"

Realizing he was fighting a losing battle, Cyrax's tone shifted from aggression to a mix of anger and self-pity. "You know why you care?" he spat at Tommy, "Because you want to fuck with the little guy that's being honest!" With these words, Cyrax abruptly left the call, leaving the hosts momentarily stunned.

In the immediate aftermath, the studio fell into a brief silence before erupting into a mix of nervous laughter and serious reflection. The hosts, still processing what had transpired, began to dissect Cyrax's behavior and the implications of his statements.

The studio atmosphere, once charged with tension, now crackled with a mix of disbelief, dark humor, and genuine concern.

Boogie2988 mused on the psychological underpinnings of Cyrax's behavior. "I think it shows the compulsion," he observed, drawing parallels to recidivist offenders on "To Catch a Predator." This comparison sparked a deeper discussion about the nature of Cyrax's apparent attraction to minors, with the hosts debating whether it stemmed from loneliness, a lack of self-confidence, or a more disturbing inherent inclination.

Tommy, still reeling from the verbal assault, maintained his stance on Cyrax's culpability. "This creep belongs in a fucking hospital like a zoo animal," he declared, his words reflecting the visceral disgust many felt towards Cyrax's alleged actions.

The conversation took an unexpected turn as the hosts delved into Cyrax's past relationships, including a transgender partner he had mentioned. This revelation led to a broader discussion about Cyrax's living situation and lack of life prospects, with the hosts struggling to understand how someone in his position could attract any romantic partners.

As the post-mortem continued, the hosts revealed additional allegations they hadn't had the chance to address during the interview. These ranged from disturbing claims about Cyrax's personal hygiene to allegations of inappropriate behavior with a blind acquaintance named Billy. The veracity of these claims remained uncertain, but they added new layers of complexity to the already troubling Cyrax saga.

The hosts also reflected on their own approach to the interview, with some expressing regret that they hadn't pushed harder on certain topics. "I wanted to let him let his guard down and then start," one host admitted, revealing the careful strategy they had attempted to employ.

As the discussion wound down, the hosts grappled with the ethical implications of their engagement with Cyrax. They questioned whether their platform had inadvertently provided him with the attention he craved, even as they sought to expose his alleged misdeeds.

## The Final Confrontation: Cyrax's Last Stand

As the LolcowLive podcast entered its final stretch, Cyrax made an unexpected return to the call, his anger barely contained. His reappearance set the stage for a final, explosive confrontation that would lay bare the depths of his delusions and the hosts' growing frustration.

Cyrax immediately launched into a defensive tirade, attempting to justify his actions by invoking law enforcement. "If I'm such an evil person," he challenged, "why is it that when I showed the police, the FBI, and the detectives, they all said that I'm not a [predator]?" This claim, repeated from earlier in the interview, was met with skepticism from the hosts.

Tommy, his patience worn thin, attempted to explain the realities of law enforcement investigations, but Cyrax's interruptions prevented any coherent discussion. The exchange quickly devolved into a shouting match, with Cyrax hurling racial slurs and personal insults at Tommy. "It's crack heads like you that I cannot respect," Cyrax spat, his face contorted with rage.

Boogie2988 tried to steer the conversation back to substantive issues, but Cyrax's aggression had reached a fever pitch. He accused the hosts of bullying him, seemingly oblivious to the irony of his own abusive language. "You waste your life, you make the people that you served with look like shit by doing shit like this," he yelled at Tommy, referencing the host's military background.

As the hosts pressed Cyrax on his use of racial slurs and his apparent hatred for certain groups, his responses became increasingly incoherent and defensive. He attempted to portray himself as a victim, claiming, "I didn't get dragged into this willingly. I got dragged into this by Music

Biz Marty who has a weird, sick obsession with me."

In a moment of unintended revelation, Cyrax admitted to making mistakes but quickly backtracked, reverting to his earlier claims of being framed or manipulated by AI technology. This inconsistency did not go unnoticed by the hosts, who continued to challenge his narrative.

The interview reached its climax when Boogie attempted to ask questions submitted by Discord members. Cyrax, realizing the nature of these questions, erupted in a final burst of profanity and threats before abruptly leaving the call for the last time.

In the aftermath of Cyrax's departure, the hosts took a moment to process the chaotic encounter. They discussed the psychological implications of Cyrax's behavior, with Boogie noting, "I'm learning a lot about humanity today." The conversation turned to broader societal issues, touching on mental health, the justice system, and the challenges of dealing with individuals like Cyrax.

While they wrapped up the episode, the hosts reflected on the ethical implications of their engagement with Cyrax. They grappled with questions of responsibility and the potential consequences of providing a platform for such controversial figures.

The episode concluded with a mix of dark humor and genuine concern. Tommy issued a final plea to Cyrax: "Just leave the kids alone, Chance. Please." This statement encapsulated the conflicting emotions stirred by the interview - a blend of disgust, pity, and a lingering hope for redemption.

While the hosts signed off, the LolcowLive studio fell into a contemplative silence. The Cyrax interview had pushed the boundaries of their format, forcing them to confront uncomfortable truths about internet culture, mental health, and the human capacity for self-deception. It left them, and their audience, with more questions than answers about the complex interplay between digital infamy and real-world consequences.

# Cyrax's Legacy and the Digital Age

We close the final pages on the saga of Chance "Cyrax" Wilkins, left to grapple with the profound implications of his story. From his humble beginnings as an aspiring musician in Akron, Ohio, to his infamous appearance on the LolcowLive podcast, Cyrax's journey serves as a stark cautionary tale for the digital age.

Cyrax's story is, at its core, a tragedy of the modern era. It is a narrative shaped by the intersection of mental health issues, the allure of internet fame, and the dark underbelly of online culture. His descent from a struggling artist to a figure of digital infamy highlights the potential dangers lurking in the vast expanses of the internet, where the line between reality and fantasy often blurs beyond recognition.

Throughout our exploration of Cyrax's life, we've witnessed a man trapped in a cycle of his own making. His desperate attempts to achieve fame and validation led him down increasingly dark paths, culminating in allegations of inappropriate behavior with minors. These accusations, whether true or exaggerated, have forever altered the course of his life and the lives of those around him.

The LolcowLive podcast appearance served as a microcosm of Cyrax's entire online existence. His inability to provide coherent explanations for his actions, his quick resort to aggression when challenged, and his persistent victimhood mentality all point to deeper psychological issues that have gone unaddressed. This final public meltdown may well mark the end of Cyrax's quest for internet stardom, but it also raises uncomfortable questions about the role of platforms that profit from the exploitation of vulnerable individuals.

Cyrax's story forces us to confront the darker aspects of internet culture. It challenges us to consider the ethics of engaging with and documenting the lives of individuals who may be struggling with mental health issues. At what point does observation become exploitation? When does the pursuit of content cross ethical boundaries?

Moreover, the Cyrax saga highlights the need for better systems to protect vulnerable individuals online, both from external threats and from their own self-destructive behaviors. It underscores the importance of digital literacy and the need for more robust mental health support systems in an increasingly connected world.

Reflecting on Cyrax's journey, we must also acknowledge the role of the broader internet community in perpetuating and escalating his behavior. The ecosystem of trolls, critics, and spectators that surrounded Cyrax played a significant part in his downfall, raising questions about collective responsibility in the digital age.

Looking to the future, the story of Cyrax serves as a powerful reminder of the potential consequences of unchecked online behavior. It challenges content creators, platforms, and audiences alike to consider the real-world impact of their digital actions.

In the end, Chance "Cyrax" Wilkins remains an enigma - a figure simultaneously pitiable and reprehensible, a product of his circumstances yet responsible for his choices. His story, while unique in its specifics, is emblematic of a broader phenomenon in the digital age: the pursuit of fame at any cost, the blurring of moral boundaries in online spaces, and the potential for the internet to amplify both the best and worst aspects of human nature.

Closing this chapter on Cyrax's life, we are left with a sobering realization: in the vast digital landscape of the 21st century, there are likely many more Cyraxes out there - individuals teetering on the edge of infamy, their stories yet to be told. It is our collective responsibility to approach these stories with empathy, critical thinking, and a commitment to fostering a healthier online environment.

The tale of Cyrax is more than just a sensational internet story; it is a mirror reflecting the complexities and challenges of life in the digital age. It compels us to examine our own online behaviors, to question the content we consume and create, and to strive for a more responsible and compassionate internet culture.

Moving forward, may the lessons learned from Cyrax's story guide us towards a more mindful and ethical engagement with the digital world. For in the end, the story of Cyrax is not just about one man's fall from grace - it is about all of us, navigating the treacherous waters of the internet age, seeking connection, validation, and meaning in a world that is increasingly mediated by screens and algorithms.

The final word on Cyrax may not yet be written, but his story will undoubtedly echo through the annals of internet history, serving as a powerful reminder of the potential pitfalls and responsibilities that come with life in the digital spotlight.

Printed in Great Britain
by Amazon

d012113b-ffb3-4a7b-b000-cdbc869e3076R02